John J. Reed

My Sabbath-School Scrap-Book

containing anniversary dialogues, addresses, recitations - in prose and verse, with

other miscellaneous pieces

John J. Reed

My Sabbath-School Scrap-Book

containing anniversary dialogues, addresses, recitations - in prose and verse, with other miscellaneous pieces

ISBN/EAN: 9783337368982

Printed in Europe, USA, Canada, Australia, Japan

Cover: Foto ©Lupo / pixelio.de

More available books at **www.hansebooks.com**

MY SABBATH-SCHOOL SCRAP-BOOK,

CONTAINING

Anniversary Dialogues, Addresses, Recitations,

ETC., ETC.,

IN PROSE AND VERSE.

WITH OTHER MISCELLANEOUS PIECES.

BY JOHN J. REED.

NEW YORK:
PUBLISHED BY TIBBALS & WHITING,
145 NASSAU STREET.
1866.

Entered, according to act of Congress, in the year 1864, by
JOHN J. REED,
In the Clerk's Office of the District Court for the Southern District of the State of New York.

TO

SABBATH-SCHOOL SUPERINTENDENTS,

ANNIVERSARY COMMITTEES,

MINISTERS AND TEACHERS, PARENTS AND CHILDREN,

AS A CONTRIBUTION

TO THE EDIFICATION OF THE YOUNG,

This Volume

IS CORDIALLY DEDICATED BY

THE AUTHOR.

PREFACE.

These pages being stereotyped and ready for the press, it is now necessary to state, briefly, the design of their publication. Two principal objects have been constantly in the writer's mind—namely: to assist in supplying the demand, which annually arises, for Sabbath-School Addresses, Dialogues, Recitations, Hymns, etc., etc.; and to add a volume to each Sabbath-School Library, which shall contain pleasing, pure and instructive Sabbath-day reading for little minds. How well these purposes have been accomplished, the reader will judge. As recitations, a few may be considered too lengthy—in which case, it will be easy for the teacher making a selection to omit sentences or paragraphs, by making a light pencil mark on the margin of the page. In some instances, the dash (———) is used, in which cases the proper name of minister, teacher, scholar, or other individual may be inserted, and thus give to the subject a local interest.

The work is what its title-page imports. It is a literal copy of "My Sabbath-School Scrap-Book"—containing a variety of pieces, written, as a general thing, on the spur of the moment, by request, or to be applied to a particular occasion. Therefore, it does not "defy the critic's dagger," but is sent forth to perform its special mission—the edification of " the little ones." It does not purport to teach the art of elocution, either in articulation or gesticulation—its end and aim being to furnish themes for the children's anniversary platforms. As such, may its words and sentiments be properly committed to memory, and rehearsed with the requisite emphasis, and the author's object will be attained.

The writer would scarcely have ventured to put these miscellanies into a book form, but the kind interest taken by friends who have used many of the productions on repeated occasions, and their desire to procure the series in a collected form, have induced him to comply with the request.

CONTENTS.

OPENING ADDRESSES.
	PAGE
Christmas Anniversary	45
Christmas Address	183
For Christmas Anniversary	193
"God is Good"	98
Special Address	15

DIALOGUES.
Disobedience to Parents	25
Ego and Echo	235
Financial	110
For a Little Boy and Girl	77
For Two Infant Class Scholars	39
"Happy New-Year"	225
"In Want of a Subject"	161
I wish I was in the Army	255
John and William's Choice	212
Money Wanted	92
On the Death of a Female Superintendent	115

	PAGE
On the Death of a Pious Scholar	143
On the Death of a Scholar	43
On the Introduction of Gas into the Church	140
Orphan Willie	80
Teachers Wanted	56
The Fatherless and Motherless	171
The Gospel Ship	218
"The Newsboy"	65
The Omnibus	205
The Sunday-School Shield	231
The Western Hunter and Atheist	237
What is that, Mother?	254

HYMNS.

Anniversary Ode	341
Christmas Hymn	90
Excursion Hymn	63
Farewell to a Pastor	337
Farewell to a Pastor	352
Hymn of Praise	139
Infant Class Hymn	169
"Little Twigs"	182
My Sabbath-School	12
New-Year Hymn	151
Pic-Nic Melody	96
Song of the Poor	179
Temperance Ode	301
Valedictory to a Pastor	344

ADDRESSES.

	PAGE
Appeal for more Teachers	33
By an Infant Scholar	55
For an Infant Scholar	112
Greeting to the Pastor	159
"Hinting at Facts"	190
My First "Extempore"	155
Responsive Address	357
Surprise Address	152
The Children's Wishes	180
Tribute on the Death of a Scholar	135
"Young America"	248

CLOSING ADDRESSES.

Christmas Address	128
For Christmas Anniversary	106
For an Infant Scholar	105
For the Times	30
New Year's Address	125

RECITATIONS.

A Message to Christians	133
Elegy	23
For an Infant Scholar	253
God	262
I'll go where Father's Gone	36
Infant Scholar's First Address	76
Little Robert Reed's Resolution	213

CONTENTS.

	PAGE
On the Death of an Aged Minister	160
On the Death of a Teacher	113
Our Pastor's Wife	157
Slander	261
"Slavery Forever!"	53
The American Boy	216
The Bible	278–283
The Closing Year	227
The Discouraged Teacher	276
The Housemaid's Soliloquy	214
The Land of the Blest	246
The Little Sunday-School Scholar	275
Though I am but a Little Boy	231
Thoughts on the Times	201
To a Mother Mourning the Loss of her Children	153
"Young America"	79
Young David's Sling and Stone	167

MISCELLANEOUS.

Acrostic	340
Dedication for an Album	355
Epitaph	290
Epitaph	48
Epitaph on a Child	211
Epitaph on a Christian Lady	200
"Fire! Fire!"	345
For the Blank Leaf of a Bible	109

CONTENTS.

	PAGE
Impromptu Lines on a Coffin-Lid	356
In Sunday-School	265
Lines in a Hymn Book	288
Lines to a Teacher	127
Our Child is Gone	339
Stanzas to a Bride	343
The Future	351
The Last Best Gift	335
The Sunday-School	245
The Sunbeams of Spring	354
To the First-Born	342
To a Sabbath Scholar	192
To a Wedded Couple	350
Tribute of Affection	347
Written in the Blank Leaf of a Bible	150

ADDITIONAL CONTENTS.

Dialogue—The Boot Black	285
Recitation—Christmas Address	290
" Jarius' Daughter	292
" "In Fogy Times"	295
Dialogue—David and Jonathan	297
Recitation—The Kiss in School	303
Colloquy—My Bible	305
Recitation—The Lost Child	316
" The Militia Captain	318
" In Memoriam	324
" Pres. Lincoln's Favorite Poem	327

My Sabbath School.

My Sabbath School.

2 Another year has passed and gone
   In Sabbath School—my Sabbath School—
Another festive day is born,
   In Sabbath School—my Sabbath School.
Fresh off'rings to the Lord to-day
Let us upon His altar lay,
Whose tender kindness strews our way
   In Sabbath School—my Sabbath School.

3 What precious seasons we have seen
   In Sabbath School—my Sabbath School!—
Where peace throughout the year has been
   In Sabbath School—my Sabbath School.
The Saviour smiles upon the place,
And lights with joy each youthful face,
Here hearts are won by saving grace—
   My Sabbath School—my Sabbath School.

4 The cause of God is gaining strength
   In Sabbath School—my Sabbath School—
And Zion's King shall reign at length,
   My Sabbath School—my Sabbath School.
Hence Bible-teachers shall go forth
To South, and East, and West, and North,
And preach "Good will" through all the earth,
   My Sabbath School—my Sabbath School.

5 Faith gives our toil-worn Teachers cheer
   In Sabbath School—my Sabbath School—
They wait the harvest to appear
   In Sabbath School—my Sabbath School.
These little ones within their care,
Now nourish'd in the house of prayer,
May early learn the Cross to bear
   In Sabbath School—my Sabbath School.

SABBATH-SCHOOL SCRAP-BOOK.

OPENING ADDRESS.

You remember, brother Hammond, when the Rebels fired their first gun, they used a far-reaching and powerful "Columbiad." They knew that a pistol-shot would be ineffectual—that it would be a mere mockery of their earnestness and hatred of our good old flag. When men wish to accomplish a purpose, they adopt the means to the end. If you intended to raise a house, you would not put a child's shoulder under the beams. You would apply some mighty lever, or screw-power. If you needed to call out the militia of the State of New-York to suppress an invasion, or announce that the "290" was coming up through the "Narrows," you would not employ a penny-trumpet—but the bugle's blast would peal through the air, and stalwart men would fly to arms! But I perceive, when you have a Sabbath-school Anniversary, you take a boy, about my size, to make *the* speech of all others the most important! Now, sir, I object—You require a Columbiad to make the people hear—to awaken in them a deeper interest in the Sabbath-school cause—to arouse them from apathy and slumber while this blessed institution demands their efforts and prayers—to make them feel that *we* too are in earnest in battering down the walls of Satan, and raising the banner of Peace in every home. But pray, sir, how far may a *boy* accomplish this? Nay, a man should deliver the Opening Address to-night—a man, whose stentorian voice would fill the church, and cause every hearer to understand that the Sabbath-school enterprise was "no child's play," but a great and glorious work, demanding their sympathy and coöperation. Notwithstanding these my objections, the Teachers have selected me to open our juvenile exercises to-night, and I will now begin, and soon end, my speech.

We assemble, kind friends, to celebrate the 28th Anniversary of the A‑‑‑‑‑‑‑-St. Sabbath-school. And oh! what hallowed memories must crowd upon the thoughts of the old veteran members of this Society, when they retrospect the past twenty-eight years! I see before me some men and women who witnessed our *first* Anniversary—but they are few, very few! The good old fathers of the Church have passed away! The sterling and unflinching men, who feared no opposition in establishing a good cause, but stood like "anvils to the stroke" in defence of Lay-representation and a Republican church, have nearly all gone to their reward. The seats they once occupied here are now filled by another generation. But their virtues and their fidelity are remembered—their steadfastness and self-sacrificing spirit in erecting this temple for God's worship, is yet honored by their successors. Their urns are filled with amaranth and evergreens. Such names as Vanhorn, and Butcher, and Scofield, and Laird, and Thompson, can never pass into oblivion.* They are immortal on earth as they are immortal in heaven.

[*A voice in the gallery:* "You did not mention William Gray, and Lockwood Smith, and Thomas Brown, and father Cook."]

No—they are living—and are "known and read of all men." They speak for themselves. I mention only a few of the "dear departed" who gave this interest its birth—to whose labors we are indebted for our beautiful little church, and who laid

* Proper names may be applied.

the foundations of the A.........-street Sabbath-school. *I* would keep their names as "familiar as a household word." Why, brother Hammond, had it not been for *those* men, we should have been deprived of your pastoral care to-day—perchance we should never have heard from your lips the story of the Cross, nor witnessed our altar surrounded by penitent ones, through your instrumentality.

My Teacher told me to be brief in my Address. "To obey is better than sacrifice," my Sunday-school Bible says—and I will try to please him. Yet, with so much to say—so much to stir the heart, and make it pulsate even quicker in these eventful times—when my country, the land of my birth, is beset with *traitors* to the best Government under the sun—where my father's flag is trampled beneath the Slaveocrat's feet, and the vile leaders of a betrayed people spurn us for our adherence to the Right—when our brothers' blood is crying from Bull-Run, and Malvern Heights, and Pea Ridge, and Fredericksburgh, and Shiloh, and Williamsburgh, and a score of battle-fields, for a just retribution and signal punishment to their *murderers*—I say, when *such* sentiments and feelings burn into the avenues of the soul, how can those fires be smothered? How can I be brief? No, sir, the shades of the fathers stand up before us—the heroes of '76 appeal to every man, woman and child in this assembly to-night, to " cut short this work in righteousness"—to banish the cause of this civil war from our borders, and plant the tree of Liberty in every State on the American Continent. Let us also, to-night, erect in our hearts a monument to the Martyrs in Humanity's great conflict, nor forget to pray for those who are weeping beside desolate hearths in widowhood and orphanage. *Human Slavery* is the grand cause of our National sorrows. A system that brutalizes the image of God—that chattelizes body and soul—that merchandizes man in a Republic of Freemen—that same system uses the same chattels as " weapons of war" to destroy our blood-cemented Union ! " It is evil and only evil." My heart sickens—my soul becomes sad, at the wrongs it has inflicted upon my country and my countrymen ; and I leave the dark canvas to your vision, while I shall look a few moments upon the brighter picture of our Sabbath-school.

And oh ! what a contrast ! How different from the scenes of strife in the outside world ! With the Bible for our text-book, we are here learning to practice the " Higher Law"—" to do unto others as we would have them do unto us." Look, friends !

upon our Sabbath-school Army. "Peace on earth and good will to man" glitters upon its banners. Its war-cry is, "Little children, love one another." Its ammunition is Truth, Mercy, Gentleness, Meekness, and the fruits of the Spirit. On one of its banners is inscribed, "Bring in the wanderers"— and we have two Missionaries, who visit from house to house, and bring in recruits. Another says, "Go ye unto all the world," and we have a Juvenile Missionary Society conducted by the children, which has realized some fifty or sixty dollars, during the last year, and is intended to do much good. It has received a beautiful and satisfactory letter from a destitute Sunday-school in Nebraska Territory, stating what benefit and cheering of hearts our donation had accomplished. We have on our roll-book —— names, and an efficient staff of officers. It would do you good, friends, to visit our Camp once in a while. You are kindly invited to look in and see us under drill, any Sabbath-day in the year. Why, just to look upon our Female Bible-class would pay you for your trouble. Nearly every one of its members have sought and found the Saviour during the past year, and are now marching forward to "the promised land." Other children also, and all but three of our good Teachers, have obtained the "pearl of great price." All of our Officers and Teachers have put on Christ as the "Captain of their salvation," and, under His leadership, hope for victory and a triumphant entrance into the Paradise of God.

It gives me pleasure to say, in closing, that God has been very good to us the past year. While the shafts of Death have made so many homes desolate, not one member of our School has been taken! Two years have passed since we made public our Anniversary, and I only remember two who have fallen within that period. One was little Harriet Young, eight years of age—a sweet bud of promise. While very sick, she would request her mother to take her from her little bed that she might get upon her knees to pray; and, when she could not be lifted from her bed, she would kneel upon it. And there was another—Mary Catharine Smith. You remember her funeral, my dear school-mates —the funeral sermon, and the church filled with sorrowful relatives and friends. Mary had been one of our scholars from her earliest childhood— had lived to become a Teacher among us—retiring and modest, loving and kind as the dove. She experienced a change of heart at this altar, when quite young—was the hope of many affectionate hearts—the light of the domestic circle, and gave promise to all for a useful life. "None knew her but to love her." But the Spoiler came, just at the dawn of womanhood. He laid his hand heavily upon her delicate frame—shook reason from its throne, and after a few months of suffering, we laid her to rest in the Union burying-ground. Sweetly she sleeps beside Elizabeth. While father and mother are weeping here to-night, she is with the angels—" my Bible tells me so."

And now, friends! hoping others who are to succeed me will prove more interesting and instructive, I will obey my father in making a *little* speech, and take my seat.

This address being local in some points, other proper names could be substituted for future use, with a few alterations.

RECITATION.

ELEGY.*

I.

Hanford! loved name! in our hearts' deep recess
It lives—to direct us, to cheer, and to bless;
"Though dead, he yet speaketh"—and, list'ning, we hear
The words of his counsel which fell on our ear.

II.

Say not he is dead!—his works and deeds live,
And the world he has honored its tribute will give;
And the seed he has sown in God's vineyard below,
By pray'rs and tears watered, shall flourish and grow.

III.

We cherish thee, Hanford! freed spirit above!
And joy in thy mem'ry as one that we love,—
Where our shepherd has gone he beckons us come,
And waits to receive us—in heaven his home.

IV.

The fold will soon follow!—with Christ for our guide,
We'll meet thee, our Hanford! and stand side by side
With the ransomed and pure—the glorified throng—
To mingle our voices in Salvation's song.

* On the death of Mr. J. E. Hanford, late Superintendent of the Fleet-St. M. E. Church Sabbath-school, Brooklyn.—Died April 5, 1863—aged 39 years.

V.

My father and mother have gone to that land,
And brothers and sisters are in the dear band,—
They'll welcome thee, HANFORD! upon the bright plain,
Where many shall say, "Thou hast not lived in vain."

VI.

Farewell! dear departed!—the race is soon run—
The battle is fought, and the victory won!
Thy weapons of warfare we'll bring to the field:
The sword of the Spirit, and Faith for our shield.

VII.

Thy grave shall be green,—ever-fragrant and blest,
By Friendship and Love with immortals be dressed,—
The myrtle—the willow—the sweet-scented rose,
Shall bloom where the ashes of HANFORD repose.

For other use, the word TEACHER can be substituted for a proper name.

DIALOGUE.

DISOBEDIENCE TO PARENTS.

BY TWO BOYS.

[*Enter Robert—a sled hung over his shoulder.*] Well, now, this is what I call a first-rate day for coasting. I guess we'll have sport and no mistake. I wish that chap would come. I'll be hanged if I like to be standing here all day, waiting for such a slow poke as he is. But here he comes. Well, we've got time to go out of town yet.

[*Enter William.*] Good morning, Robert. I see you are prepared to go coasting. Where do you intend to go?

R. Out of town, to be sure.

W. I am afraid then, Robert, that I cannot accompany you, for father told me that I must not go far from home; and I know that your father does not want you to go, either.

R. Oh, cracky! Ain't you old enough to take care of yourself? I should like to have my old man to tell me so. I'd go in spite of him—I can tell you that.

W. You cannot think it would be very proper for you to disobey your father, certainly.

R. Oh, I don't know as it's going to hurt the old man, if I do go out for an hour or two.

W. That is not the thing. Your father has forbidden you going; and if you should disobey him, you would be doing that which is very wicked.

R. Oh, you get out. It's enough to make a fellow sick to hear you talk. You put me in mind of an old woman.

W. It may be very well for you to talk so now; but supposing some dreadful punishment should be sent upon you for your disobedience. Did you ever hear of the Children of Israel?

R. Children of Israel? Let me see. No; I don't know as I ever did. What of them?

W. Well, on account of certain acts of disobedience in the wilderness, the plague of fiery serpents was sent upon them.

R. If them children were green enough to let "old Israel" know what they had been about, they did deserve to be licked. But what kind of a plague was sent on them? Fiery serpents, did you say?

W. Flying fiery serpents, which stung the people so that they died in great numbers.

R. Died! You don't mean to say that the serpents killed them?

W. Yes they did, though, and all on account of disobedience.

R. Well, I'm blowed if that wasn't hard enough. Now I don't see why "old Israel" didn't lick them and have done with it; and if they didn't mind that, he could have come some other game over them.

W. You seem to have a wrong idea of the children of Israel. They were the chosen people of God, but were nevertheless very wicked and rebellious people, and God found it necessary sometimes to deal with them harshly.

R. Oh that's it, is it?

W. Yes, and as I was saying, you might be visited with some punishment on account of your disobedience to your father.

R. No I won't though, for I needn't tell the old man, and then he wouldn't know anything about it.

W. But if your father shouldn't know it, you would be none the less guilty in the sight of God—

R. Oh, never mind about that.

W. ——— Who has said, "Honor thy father and——

R. Oh, humbug! I'm going out of town; and

if you ain't going, just say so. I ain't going to stand here all day talking to you; but I'll tell you what it is—you'd better go.

W. No, Robert, I cannot. I know that I would be doing wrong to disobey my father.

R. Now couldn't you tell him that you had been somewhere else—say you had been down to see some of the boys.

W. That would be telling a falsehood.

R. Oh, what of that?

W. A great deal of it. It is very wicked to tell stories. Did you ever read in the Bible of Ananias and Sapphira?

R. Ananias who?

W. Ananias, and Sapphira, his wife, who told stories, and were struck dead on the spot for their wickedness.

R. Oh, when a man and his wife go to telling lies, it's a different thing. *They* ought to know better.

W. It is as wicked for you to tell lies as for them, and you might be punished for it in the same way, for all you know.

R. Well, now, look here. Is that true you're telling me, or are you only gasing?

W. It is quite true, Robert. You may read it for yourself, in the Bible.

R. Oh, you read it in the Bible? Well, if it's a fact, I'm kinder of the opinion that folks might as well not tell lies and be disobedient.

W. That is just what I wish you to understand; and if you will come to our Sunday-school next Sunday morning, I will show you in the Bible, the things I have been telling you.

R. Will you? Well, I'll come; and if you say so, we'll go round to our house now, and try our sleds on the sidewalk.

W. I have no objection to do that, and even if our sport shouldn't be so good as it might be in some other place, we'll have the satisfaction of knowing that we are not enjoying ourselves at the expense of disobedience to our parents.

R. Well, let's go.

CLOSING ADDRESS.

BY A BOY.

I rise, Mr. Chairman, just briefly to say
That our school-exercises are closed for to-day—
My speech comes the last, as your programme will show,
"The last and the least" you will very soon know.
Before you retire, please give your attention
To the few little items I purpose to mention.

I feel patriotic, and ready to fight!
But 'tis not the place, nor is it the night:
And yet, when I think of the friends we hold dear,
Whose presence was wont our school-room to cheer—
Of our fathers and brothers encamped on the field
To defend the old flag, and its glory to shield;
Of the " Christmas " *they* spend in an enemy's land,
Where hardships and dangers and death are at hand;
Where the cold winter storm and the comfortless tent
Discover the horrors the traitors have sent
On our once peaceful nation, the best 'neath the sun—
My spirit *will* rouse, and I want to be one
Of its million defenders—to strike for the Right,
And banish Secession forever from sight—
To punish the Rebels with bullet-hole scars,
And make their vile leaders return us our Stars.
But this is unchristian—I hear a Voice say,
" Vengeance is mine, and I will repay."

We'll remember our soldiers—and pray God to bless
The cause of the Union, and grant them success;
We'll pray for our soldiers, that Peace may soon come,
When the heart of the North shall welcome them home.

  Alas! for the war, with its evils untold,
Its postage-stamp issues for silver and gold—
Its fabulous prices, and still on the rise,
Make poor people wonder and open their eyes;
The revenue bills and the taxes on trade,
Exceed all the "panics" that ever were made!
If such be the mischief this conflict attends,
Pray, what will it do before the war ends?

  Thus endeth the chapter. But you will perceive
The "machine" is still moving, and I cannot leave.
The evening has pass'd, and our songs have been sung,
Imparting delight to the old and the young:
You've heard our recitals, and dialogues too,
And remember the moral each piece had in view.
How well we have spoken and acted our part,
Our friends can best judge—with a liberal heart.
Much praise should be given, much credit is due
To the untiring labors of Mr. Cocheu,—
As also friend Piersall, so kind and so clever,
Has made our improvement his highest endeavor:
With him for our General throughout the past year,
These little cadets have had nothing to fear.

His Sabbath-day "rations" have been the best kind,
Good cheer for the heart and good food for the mind.
Our camp has been pleasant—our Chaplain you know,
Who carries no ARMS, but can face any foe
With the sword of the Spirit, and much he has done
To conquer a peace since his warfare begun.
Our Teachers, God bless them! we cannot forget—
They've toiled on for years, and remain with us yet;
Unwearied in duty, like sentinels stand
These brave volunteers in the Sabbath-school band.
Oh! give them your blessing, ye lovers of Truth!
Ye fathers and mothers who cherish our youth!
Oh! give them your prayers, that long they may live
To sow the good seed which a harvest shall give.

And now I must close. Your patience has fled,
And these "little folk" should be snugly in bed.
In the name of the School, and its managers all,
We thank you for making this annual call.
With hearty good wishes I now leave your sight,
And many hearts join me in saying "Good-night!"

ADDRESS.

APPEAL FOR MORE TEACHERS.

BY A BOY.

Beloved Assembly:

It is my privilege, in the order of Providence, to appear before you on this interesting occasion, as the * * * * Sabbath-school representative. A task is before me to which I am unaccustomed, and feel incapable of performing. I have no pride to gratify, and had I not been chosen for this department of the exhibition, would have been content with a private seat. But I have been taught that " to obey is better than sacrifice." My instructions were, to inform the congregation that we are frequently embarrassed for the want of teachers— to inform you of what you all know, though some may forget, that a school implies teaching, and that a school without teachers is no school. Do not understand me, my friends, that *our* school is without teachers ! No—so far from it, we have them of years' standing—judicious and persevering. We have some, I believe, who would think themselves sinning were they absent a day—and some whom these, my companions, would conclude they were sick should they leave them. Flattery, my friends, is no part of my nature, but "honor to whom honor is due." The Sabbath-school is called "an excellent institution"—the Sabbath-day nursery"—"the church's garden"—"the bulwark of Christianity." We hear it lauded—praised—admired—and sorry am I to finish the sentence with —NEGLECTED. This school has about one hundred scholars. Remember, friends, one hundred immortal minds that will meet you in the judgment—one hundred who are rising up to fill the seats vacated by our fathers in the church. The number of teachers is about —— but perhaps it's best not to tell—come next Sabbath morning, dear friend, and count them for yourself. We have a large room for our school, fitted for as many more scholars. And should any feel disposed to accept a teacher's office, no doubt our present teachers would be willing, many of them, to go through alley and street and lane for children, and our school might soon be filled. My business to-night is, to ask for volunteers. We are here drilling soldiers to battle against the King's enemies—we are here training seamen for the old ship Zion—we are here, perhaps, preparing missionaries to the heathen who are sitting in darkness and the shadow of death—we are here chiseling pillars to uphold the church militant. In order to this, we ask for help—such help as will stand by us—help that will not grow "weary in well doing." In the name of the orphans' and widows' God, I present our Sabbath-school to His friends. "Parents, teachers, help us, onward as we go." Here is work that must be done—here are children eager for instruction—here are young immortals who are looking up to the Church as their fostering parent, who may become her shining lights, and hail you her members in the "harvest home" as instruments of their salvation. Behold them, Christians! behold them, ye who would add glory to the Lord's anointed—behold them, the "lambs of the fold." (*All rise.*) These, these are the subjects of my appeal, and in their behalf your speaker asks for aid. It is yours to lead them in the way everlasting—it is yours to see them rising up and call you blessed—it is yours to make them happy here and happy hereafter—it is yours to lead them into " green pastures and beside the still waters." And it is yours to say whether I need longer ask for teachers—teachers—teachers.

RECITATION.

I'LL GO WHERE FATHER'S* GONE.

BY A GIRL.

I HAVE one friend—a faithful friend,
    Beside my little brother—
With her my happiest hours I spend,
    My kind and cherished mother.
I often see her falling tears,
    And mark her bosom swelling,
While she is thinking of the years
    When sunshine filled our dwelling.

We're lonely now---our little cot
    Has lost its former gladness—
The Past can never be forgot,
    Though Mem'ry brings us sadness.

---

* Referring to the death of Mr. Joseph Lisk, late Superintendent of Grand-St. M. P. Church Sabbath-school.

I can remember well the voice
   Which cheered our hours at even—
Which made our infant hearts rejoice,
   And made our home a heaven.

My father then was always near
   To soothe me and my brother;
His kindly words and looks of cheer
   Brought comfort to my mother.
Beside his chair, and on his knee,
   He told us of the Saviour—
And godly precepts gave to me
   To guide in my behavior.

He used to sing of "heaven his home,"
   The land where he was going—
Where Death, he said, could never come,
   Nor farewell tears are flowing:
And he has gone!—our household band
   By Death's rude touch is broken;
No more we take our father's hand,
   His last " good night" is spoken.

Mother! we'll meet him by and bye,
   In climes of endless pleasure—
And then, dear brother, you and I
   Will see our earth-lost treasure.

A few brief years—they'll not be long—
　　We'll join the saints in glory,
And mingle in Salvation's song,
　　And Love's redeeming story.

I'll go where father's gone—no more
　　Shall Sorrow's tears be falling;
He waits to meet us on Life's shore,
　　And Jesus' voice is calling.
I'll go where father's gone, and see
　　Those mansions bright and fair—
Come, school-mates, will you go with me?
　　Oh! shall I see you there?

DIALOGUE.

BY TWO INFANT CLASS SCHOLARS.

Caroline. Come up, brother John! come up! I want to talk with you.

John. Coming, sister Caroline! but couldn't you "talk with me" without getting way up here?

Caroline. Oh yes, brother John! but the good people have come to *see* as well as *hear;* and you should gratify them. I want to know if *you* go to Sabbath-school, brother John!

John. Certainly I do—and regular too.

Caroline. Where is your school, brother John?

John. Our school! why, every body ought to know that. Our school is in A........ Street, between D......... and R............, just above the watch-house, and most every body knows where that is.

Caroline. How long have you been going to school?

John. A good while—I guess a year.

Caroline. Why should a little boy like you go to Sabbath-school?

John. Mother sends me, and I go because I love to go.

Caroline. Why do you love to go?

John. Because I there hear of God and heaven—and I learn to read and sing, and it's a good place to spend the Lord's day.

Caroline. But you are too little,—ain't you in the way?

John. Not I—"It's the mind that makes the man"—and being little, I don't take much room.

Caroline. Where do they put you, Johnny, in the corner?

John. No, no, I belong to the Infant Class, and we have plenty of room for a good many more.

Caroline. How many infants have you there, Johnny? Are there any more as small as you?

John. Here they are, you may count them for yourself. (C. counts, 1, 2, 3.)

Caroline. (Telling the No.) Quite a family of little brothers and sisters. Do you want any more, Johnny? I guess I'll come too.

John. Do come, sister Caroline! we want all we can get. We will teach you to read and sing, and show you the way to be happy here and happy hereafter.

Caroline. I want to know, Johnny! if you little

folks can sing! I should like to hear you. What do you sing?

John. Why, we sing " sacred music," to be sure. And if you will promise to join our school, I'll get the scholars to sing for you.

Caroline. Well, I will, Johnny, if you sing good enough.

John. Come, school-mates, show Caroline what you can do, and let us get another scholar in the Infant Class.

(*Children Rise.*)

Where, oh! where, is good old Daniel?
    Safe in the promised land—
He went there through the den of lions,
    Safe in the promised land.

Where, oh! where are the Hebrew children?
    Safe in the promised land—
They went there through the fiery furnace,
    Safe in the promised land.

Chorus. By and by we'll go home and meet them.

Where, oh! where are Paul and Silas,
    Safe in the promised land—
They sang praises while in prison,
    Now in the promised land.

Where, oh! where is the praying mother?
    Safe in the promised land:
She went there through tribulation—
    Safe in the promised land.

Chorus. By and by we'll go and meet them.

Caroline. Pretty good! now, Johnny, you call for me next Sunday, and we will both go together, and I will try to get Samuel, and Jane, and Louisa, and Mary to come too, if I like it. So good evening, brother John.

John. Good night, Caroline. (*Goes to the stairs.*)

(*A little Girl.*) But stop, brother John! don't be in such a hurry! Can't you sing that little hymn about Moses for us?

John. (*hems.*) If the children will join in, I will help.

(*All sing.*)

(John, going to the steps. *A girl*)—Johnny, did you see the plates? I don't believe we've got money enough!

John. No, I didn't look. But I guess you did. I never peep at the plates like some folks. If there ain't enough, we can have more. Mr. B——, have you got money enough? (No.) Do you hear that, friends? Just "fork over."

DIALOGUE.

ON THE DEATH OF A SCHOLAR.

Child. Dear mother! where is Hannah Weeks?
    I thought to see her here—
And when the Class of Infants speaks,
    I thought she'd there appear.

    Has the cold weather kept her home?
        Or is she sick a bed?
Moth. No, child! the reason she don't come
    Is simply this—she's dead!

Child. When did she die, dear mother, say?
    It can't be long ago—
I saw her here last New-Year's day,
    And she was well you know.

Moth. Yes, daughter! two brief months have sped,
    Since she was here in bloom!
She sicken'd quick—and quickly fled—
    A tenant of the tomb.

Child. But, mother! did she not intend
    To sing with us this year?
How could she leave each little friend,
    When Christmas was so near?

Moth. God call'd her, child!--He knows what's best
    For all the human race--
She now is singing with the blest
    In yonder happy place.

  And tho' each little school-mate weeps,
    And parents often sigh--
Remember, Hannah only sleeps--
    Good children never die.

Child. Well, mother, I am glad to know
    That Hannah cannot die;
And I'll be good, that I may go
    And sing with her on high.

Moth. Yes, child! attend your Sabbath School,
    And mind your teachers well;
Take *this* blest volume for your rule,
    And you with her may dwell

OPENING ADDRESS.

CHRISTMAS ANNIVERSARY.

Mr. Superintendent:

I notice in your Programme that *my* name is announced as your first speaker. I thank you for the compliment, sir; but I really think your preference is unadvised. It is not the practice of "Young America" to back down at trifles—and it shall not be *me* to say I cannot be "the first speaker"—and, with your forbearance, indulgent auditors, I will now occupy a few moments of precious time.

But, wherewithal shall I make a beginning? It is a Sabbath-school Anniversary—and this, it strikes me, should be my theme—"*Our Sabbath School.*" Its history is written in many hearts—its influence is felt in many homes to-night. It is true our numbers are small—our school-room is small—our Society is small—the receipts for our Anniversary may be small, and our kind Teachers be obliged to "foot the bill" as they have done before; yet we are not disposed to despise "the day of small things," but intend to-night to make "Merry Christmas" for our Sabbath-school children in Dialogues, Recitations, and songs of praise. But why should we call ourselves *small*? Can a united band of little brothers and sisters—a united band of Teachers and Scholars—properly be called small? Not so! Robert Raikes opened his first Sabbath-school in Gloucester, England, with five little boys and girls —it was a small beginning—but by unity and steadfast endeavor the seed thus sown has borne fruit a thousand-fold. The great German Reformer —Luther—single-handed and alone, contended against the Pope of Rome and his emissaries and the King and nobles of his country. He had found the Word of God in his cloister—that book kindled in his heart the flame of heavenly love ; and with its fires burning, he went forth proclaiming the unsearchable riches of Christ. Through his perseverance, *we* enjoy the results of the Protestant Reformation. And do you call them *small*? When Mr. Wesley organized his first little church, and preached to the people the Saviour's missionary doctrine, to "Go ye into all the world, beginning at Jerusalem," was it even presumable that Methodism would then and there have its birth ? Truly the beginning was small, but great and glorious have been the benefits. So in our little vineyard—the few plants and tender flowers we have under culture are growing up and putting forth in our Sabbath garden. The buds will soon be blossoms, and the fruit will appear by-and-by. These vineyard dressers (our Sabbath-school Teachers) are, many of them, the seedlings of our Sabbath-school, who have been trained by other hands, and they remain to do the blessed work. That work is to cultivate the hardened soil of the heart—to plant the seeds of Gospel truth in these young minds—to entwine these little tendrils around the Cross—to root out the seeds of error and infidelity and sin. It is a work to fill an angel's hands—it is employment to engage the Christian's heart. I will not call it small—for " great will be your reward in heaven." God has given it His sanction, and His blessing will follow you, kind teachers ! You have heeded the Master's injunction : " Feed my lambs" —and He will be your sure reward. *We* cannot compensate you for your toil and " labor of love " —for your patience with our waywardness. The fruit awaits you in the bright hereafter. Heaven will reveal it. Oh ! then, be not weary in well-doing, for the promise is plain—" Ye *shall* reap if ye faint not." It is a promise made by our Maker.

It comes from heaven to stimulate you when weary. It comes from God—the

> "God of our childhood—God of our youth,
> God never erring—God of all truth—
> God of the sunshine—God of the storm,
> God of the springtime, joyous and warm,
> God of the winter, its frost and its blast,
> God of the present, future, and past;
> God of the Bible, Sabbath, and rest,
> God of our School, so signally blest;
> God our defense, by day and by night,
> God our Redeemer—Leader and Light."

Now permit me to make a few remarks more intimately connected with the school. Many have been the changes since last we met to celebrate its Anniversary. Our former excellent Superintendent, Mr. H——, left here last September for England, and has not returned. The call of the President for volunteers has been responded to by a former Superintendent, our Secretary, Librarian, and two of our Teachers. They felt it to be a Christian duty to obey "the powers that be" as the voice of God—to defend the "Flag of the Free" against the insults of slave-masters and political aspirants for power. They sprang to arms to sustain the Constitution and the Laws—have mingled in many skirmishes and conflicts on the bloody fields of Virginia ; and yet, to the present time, not one has sustained any serious injury. God has had them in his care—it may be in answer to prayer, for even the children pray for their friends in this "strife of arms," and they are not forgotten by the church. May God speedily return them to us again!

In connection with our Sabbath-school, we have an organized Temperance Society, which has its stated meetings, where the children enjoy singing and speaking, and pledge themselves to shun the intoxicating bowl. This influence for good may not be estimated. It will "grow with their growth, and strengthen with their strength"—and, rising into manhood, the early established principles of temperance will follow them, we trust, though useful lives. To-night we lament the loss of one of our little boys. In August last, J—— E—— was in his class on Sunday, bright and cheerful, and during the week was accidentally shot with a pistol in the hands of a playmate. In a body the school followed his remains to the grave-yard. He has early escaped from "the evil to come" and left his companions behind. In September, two of our little girls were taken from us in one short week : L—— G—— from the Infant Class, and Catharine —— from the Youths' Department. The circumstances connected with the death of the latter is an argument in favor of fostering our Juvenile Temperance Society. The child was very sick, but able to sit up, and was at the tea-table when her father came home intoxicated. After some hard words with his wife, he struck her in the face! Upon seeing this brutality, little C—— sprang between her mother and father, and was immediately taken with a fit of coughing blood, which continued until she had coughed her life away! Her last utterances were, "Jesus said, Suffer little children to come unto me," from which her afflicted mother and two little sisters derive the consoling faith that He has taken her to a better home in heaven.

> "They have gone to the tomb!
> Immortality's lamp burns bright 'mid the gloom—
> But glad is the dawn, soon to follow the night,
> When the sun-rise of glory shall beam on their sight;
> When the full matin-song, as the sleepers arise,
> To shout in the morning, shall peal through the skies."

At the close of the year 1862, we come together to celebrate the birth of the world's Redeemer, in the capacity of a Sabbath-school. How great is the privilege we enjoy! How much of blessing, even amidst the ravages of civil war, have we to be grateful to God for! The Gospel of Christ is proclaimed among us, announcing pardon and peace to the guilty and the vile—the Bible is ours, to point the way to obtain "eternal life" and a blissful existence beyond the grave—the Sabbath is ours, to rest from toil and wearisome care, and worship God according to the dictates of conscience—free institutions, freedom of speech and freedom of the press are ours—the Sabbath-school, thanks be to the Saviour, is ours, wherein the children may come and be taught the rudiments of a pure Christianity, and be prepared to "vindicate the ways of God to men." Oh! let us be thankful! Let us work for God and for souls "while it is called to-day." Let the church awake from apathy, and labor more to bring the children into Christ's fold. Do you realize, fathers and mothers, that *these* little ones are to become your successors in the church when you shall leave it for the church triumphant? To this end, they *must* be brought up "in the fear and admonition of the Lord." To accomplish this, the Sabbath-school is a heaven-appointed instrumentality. Had I a trumpet voice, I would call upon the church to awake to this subject—I would call upon the ministry for more help in this field of labor. Oh, Brother W...... ! let your voice be heard in our behalf—make *strong* and *loud* appeals for this little " nursery of the church." When your work is done, veteran soldier of the Cross—when you " rest from your labors, your work will follow you ;" and when at last, Pastor and Teachers and Children reunite in God's everlasting kingdom, may many hail you as their spiritual father, brought to Christ in the G......-St. Sabbath-school.

Dec. 25th, 1862.

RECITATION.

"SLAVERY FOREVER"!

BY A BOY

And is it so? Say, is it so?
   Speak out, my country, speak!
I wish the solemn truth to know,
   For blushes burn my cheek—
Do SIN and WRONG these States cement?
And are we in our bonds content?

Speak, PLYMOUTH ROCK! didst ever hear
   The Mayflower heroes say
That this New World, to them so dear,
   Should groan with slaves one day,
And that, in a few later years,
Their sons should dwell 'mid bondmen's tears?

Speak, BUNKER HILL! was this the aim,
   For which thy warriors bled—
To gain for FREEDOM but a name
   When they were with the dead?
Does thy proud pillar, high in air,
This shameful mockery declare?

Speak, PATRIOT SIRES! ye brave and wise!
   Ye sterling men of yore!
Did Slavery's growth and giant rise
   Engross your Council floor?
Did ye foresee in Seventy-six,
Your Colonies in "such a fix?"

Is this the fruit of all your toil,
   Our father—WASHINGTON—
To give to Slavery the soil
   Which thy brave heart has won?
Is this the sequel of thy pains
To bind our countrymen in chains?

And say, proud FLAG! my Nation's Flag!
   Escutcheon of the Free!
Emblem of which all Yankees "brag"
   And boast their Liberty—
Dost thou from fort and tower declare
All men shall thy protection share?

Speak, STATESMEN, speak! is this broad land
   Preserv'd by human wrongs?
And do ye fellowship the hand
   Which this dire curse prolongs?
Do ye in Congress hold a place,
And vote for fetters—shame—disgrace?

Speak out, ye ballots of the free!
    Shall this vile scourge increase?
Shall we to Slavery bow the knee,
    Or shall its inroads cease?
Shall SUMTER's walls be rent and riven,
    And Freedom fall? Prevent it, Heaven!
April, 1861.

APPEAL FOR MISSIONS.

BY AN INFANT SCHOLAR.

Mr. President:

  The people here will think it strange
    To see *me* on the stage,
  But as you are in want of *change*,
    I heart and soul engage
  To get some money, if I can,
  To carry out your mission plan.

  Come, then, dear friends! we want it bad,
    And feel assured we'll get it—
  'Twill make the heathen children glad,
    And you will not regret it.
  Your kindness none will underrate,
  So put your dollars in the plate.

DIALOGUE.

"TEACHERS WANTED."

BY A BOY AND A GIRL.

Matthew.—Happy New Year, Margaret Ann. I rejoice to find you participating in the annual celebration of our Sabbath-school this evening, and trust that much good will spring from it. I see many here to-night who are warm friends of our school, and who have stood by it "through thick and thin"—and some are here who profess much interest in the cause, but for some reason or other they only visit us once a year when the "children are to speak." I hope such won't be affronted if they overhear me.

Margaret Ann.—Well, Matthew, I'm obliged to you for wishing me a Happy New Year, and cheerfully return you the same. But let me tell you, Matthew, that if you expect me to hold a dialogue with you, I want to know what subject you propose, that we may not wander in our conversation "as the manner of some is." I should judge from the way you began, that you meant to read a lecture to " those whom it may concern."

Matthew.—I have no lecture to read, Margaret; but would simply ask you why a notice was read in this pulpit a few Sundays ago, stating that Teachers were needed in our school? Was it not because our professed friends do not come to see whether our Superintendent is supplied with teachers? I thought when that notice was read, how few of the Saviour's professed followers do whatsoever their hands find to do—to say nothing of doing it with their might. How few who praise and extol Sabbath-school instruction, really believe it as beneficial as they pretend. Perhaps some think, however, that to enter the door, and seat their children on a bench, is sufficient, so long as they are out of the street. And some, perhaps, think they do all that is required of them, if they give our Superintendent and teachers the privilege and honor of instructing their " little responsibilities." Wonder if such ever think of their children after they leave home on the Sabbath until they return again! Wonder if they ever ask God's blessing on the seed that is sown in their young minds, that it may bring forth fruit to his glory!

Margaret Ann.—Why, Matthew, what's the matter with you? You seem a little out of humor, don't you? I hope you'll feel better by and by, however. For my part I expect to see a glittering, *shining* interest manifested here to-night.

Matthew.—You mean in dollars and cents, I suppose. Well, that's very good, so far as it goes. But isn't wisdom far above silver and gold? What though we had all the gold of Ophar in our school, and had not teachers to impart instruction—would it be a school? No. What though the church say the Sabbath-school is its hope of future prosperity —and yet the church neglect it—will not its hope prove delusive and its prosperity suffer loss? I believe that that denomination which best fosters and cherishes its own Sabbath-schools, will best increase in strength and numbers, and carry with them the impurest or holiest influences. And I would ask, if the Papist Church is not awake on this subject? Ask her if she wants teachers in this department. No—they feel and understand its importance, and heart and hand and head are engaged.

Margaret Ann.—You are quite a moralist, Matthew. But why all this lamentation and complaint? Do not our folks duly appreciate the Sabbath-school enterprise! I'm sure whenever we have an exhibition, the church is well filled, and most everybody has got his hands in his pocket to help it forward. Beside, I often hear the pastor pray in public for its success—and the people say amen to it. Beside, at our monthly prayer-meeting one or two of the members are generally present. I hope you don't mean we are entirely neglected.

Matthew.—I don't feel alone in my complaint. The Macedonian cry for help is often heard, not only in this, but in other schools. And why is it? Are not the souls of the children as imperishable as those of the parents? Are they not soon to take their places, and when they are sleeping the sleep of death, shall they be incompetent to defend the principles and truths of their fathers and their God? Shall not the succeeding generations of this proud and favored city be wiser even in the things of God than their predecessors? They may. The experience and intelligence of the fathers may be imparted to their children before they leave them to the scoffs and buffetings of a semi-infidel world—and oh! what a rich legacy! to have the mind so imbued with biblical truth that we may " persuade men to be Christians," and thus help them on to glory and immortal life! Better far than houses and lands—better far to be heirs of God than heirs to the kingdoms and crowns of men.

Margaret Ann.—I think so myself, Matthew. I had rather when father and mother die, they would leave me with a Bible, and a saving acquaintance with its truths, than to be left with riches, and my mind unadorned with the precepts of the Gospel as taught in the Sabbath-school. "Riches take to themselves wings and fly away." As said Agar so say I—" Give me neither poverty nor riches."—Give me understanding rather—let me believe that " my bread and water shall be sure"—that when life's sundown comes, and these eyes are fixed in death—when the friends of my household close the coffin-lid, and leave me in my shroud alone—and these now active limbs are mouldering in the dust —let me know that in heaven I shall rest—that I shall behold my God in peace—and it is all I crave. Yes, Matthew, wisdom is far before rubies.

Matthew.—So says Solomon. But the Solomons of our day seem to hold the doctrine to " get all they can, and keep all they get." Many are the members of this congregation well qualified to impart instruction in the Sabbath-school, who can hear an appeal for teachers, yet feel unmoved. Yes, there are young men here, and women too, who have no "wants but what themselves create"—who from their actions had rather see children prowling our streets, or hear that they were seated in a Sabbath-school waiting for tutors, than lose three hours in their "day of rest."

Margaret Ann.—I confess, Matthew, that to see a class of children waiting for a teacher, looks very strange to me. Why, the heathen would laugh at it outright, and set it down as the eighth wonder in the world. And what must the stoic and skeptic think! How must they look upon that church whose Sabbath-school is languishing for want of teachers! Mercy on me! how much colder and harder their hearts must get, when a notice is read—" Teachers wanted here for one, two or three classes of Sabbath-school children!"

Matthew.—And did you ever think, Margaret Ann, how the children themselves must feel?—They no doubt hurry their mothers to get breakfast, that they may not be too late—perhaps they come through "rain and sleet and driving snow,"—they take their accustomed seat, and there they sit and sit—and now the bell rings—" close your books" is heard from the desk—" first class go into church" —there, they are all seated—the benediction is pronounced, and they return home, George to tell his mother he knew as much as when he went, and William to tell his father "he guessed his teacher was afraid of the snow."

George. (in the congregation). I didn't tell mother so, Matthew. I should be ashamed to let mother know that I'ze no teacher to learn me the letters.

William.—Nor I, Matthew. Father wouldn't like to hear it, for the credit of the church.

Margaret Ann.—Well, Matthew, as your lecture has spun out pretty long, I now propose that you give way to something more agreeable. It is good advice you know, Matthew, " never to speak when you have nothing to say, and always stop when you have done."

Matthew.—I have a good deal more to say, Margaret, but will defer it if you think best: and if you feel interested enough, I may finish my " lecture" as you call it, at another time. Good evening, Margaret Ann.

Margaret Ann.—Farewell, Matthew.

EXCURSION HYMN.

Tune—" YE BANKS AND BRAES O' BONNY DOON."

WELCOME, dear children! hail the day
   On which we leave the City's shore!
Bright Phœbus comes to light our way,
   And gild the waves we're passing o'er.
We flee the heat—the din—the strife—
   The studies of our school and home:
Farewell, ye daily scenes of life,
   Once more our festive day has come!

Like birds uncaged, we'll gain the air,
   And seek some green, sequester'd shade,
Where wild flow'rs bloom, and Nature fair
   Proclaims "the country GOD hath made."
We'll joy and sing from boat and barge,
   And drink the breeze which Ocean sends;
And while our eyes our hearts enlarge,
   We'll love the more our teacher-friends.

Proud River! on thy bosom bear
    This precious freight—this happy band—
Thy varied grandeurs may we share,
    And trace the great Creator's hand.
God in His works we come to see—
    God in the woods and fields to view—
Our praise shall rise in harmony,
    And Echo shall our song pursue.

Come, school-mates! join the glad acclaim,
    Let Music have a soul to-day!
Together bless our Father's name,
    And seek His guidance on our way.
He made the sea—the hills—the grove—
    The trees put forth at His command;
Whilst we, the children of His love,
    Are kept by His controlling hand!

Now let our thanks and blessings blend
    Upon our Teachers—faithful—kind—
Divine Instructor! send, oh! send
    Thy love and peace to every mind.
May Heaven's smile their toils repay,
    Until to Zion all shall come—
And meet in that great triumph day,
    To shout with Raikes the "harvest home!"

DIALOGUE.

"THE NEWSBOY."

BY TWO BOYS AND A GIRL.

[*Enter* PETER (*hastily*) *on one side and* WILLIAM *at the other.*]

William. How now, Peter? what is the matter? you seem to be all out of breath.

Peter. [*puffing and blowing*]. Whew! and so would you, if you had been running a footrace with a Sunday officer. Blame my buttons, if it don't make a fellow blow like blazes!

William. I suppose you mean that you have been conducting yourself in such a manner that a Sunday officer found it necessary to correct you.

Peter. Conductin' how? Can't a fellow stand on a corner, and smoke a segar, without havin' a blamed Sunday officer come at him with a rattan?

William. I presume that you must have been annoying the people as they were passing by.

Peter. Oh, you shut up! I never see such a fellow as you! But you needn't try to come round me with your gas,—I'll do as I've a mind to, on Sunday the same as on any other day : and if that blamed old sucker of a Sunday officer don't let me be—I'll give him fits—now mind I tell ye.

William. For shame! Peter! how can you talk in that manner? Do you not know that it is very wicked to resist the authority of the " powers that be ?"

Peter. Powers be hanged! what kind of a " power " do you call old " Snooks" any how—with his old white hat, monkey jacket, and rattan? Power! eh? well, that's pretty good,—ha! ha! ha! Well, all I know is, that he needn't try to come his power over me and the " boys," or he'll catch " Jesse."

William. I fear there is little hope in arguing the matter with you, Peter. The evil company with which you have of late associated, seems to have contaminated your mind, and I am sorry to find that you are not the boy you once was, when you went to our Sabbath-school, a few years since.

Peter. I shouldn't think I was! I know better than waste my time pokin' over Bible lessons and studyin' proofs. A chap has enough to do to go to school week days (although I don't do much of that now,) let alone goin' to church, and Sabbath-school on Sundays. Oh, gammon! Bill! you can't come it over this child [*putting his thumb to his nose*] no how.

William. My dear Peter, I wish I could impress upon you the wickedness of your course, and induce you once more to make one of our happy number in Sabbath-school. Tell me candidly, was you not happier when attending our school, than you have ever been since in loafing about the streets, and setting at defiance the laws of God and man?

Peter. Oh, well, that's neither here nor there— I'm bound to have my fun, so you may stop your preaching and "tote" yourself along.

William. But, Peter——

Peter. [*Interrupting him, and threatening to strike him*]. Shut up, I tell you, or I'll let you have a sockdolager, that'll spoil that long deacon's face of yours. But here comes Dick Wheeler—I'll set *him* at you.

[*Dick Wheeler is discovered coming up the aisle dressed in the character of a ragged newsboy, with a bundle of papers under his arm—crying "Here's the Sunday Herald, Sunday Atlas—Mercury and Noah's Weekly Messenger."*]

William. Neither you nor "Dick Wheeler," as

you call him, can intimidate me in what I conceive to be my duty—so I shall wait and talk to him also.

[*Enter Dick Wheeler, crying his newspapers.*]

Peter. Halloh, Dick ! what's the word—sold plenty o' papers this morning ?

Dick. Plenty o' papers ! No ! I'll get *stuck* as sure as my name's Dick Wheeler, if I don't get rid of them pretty sudden.

Peter. Oh, Dick—here's a fellow been talkin' to me about goin' to Sabbath-school. Ain't he green ?

Dick. I should think he was. What did you tell him ?

Peter. I *telled* him to go to grass, I was goin' to have my fun, and go where I pleased, Sundays as well as other days. [*slapping him on the back.*]

Dick. That's you, I glory in your spunk. [*Turning to William.*] So you calculated to come it over Pete, with your gassy nonsense, did you ?

[*Peter takes out his marbles and commences playing, while William and Dick conduct the dialogue.*]

William. You may call my conduct and conversation what you please, my young friend—but let me tell you as I did Peter, that you are in the "broad road that leads to death," and if you do not forsake your evil ways, you will yet bitterly regret it. I pray God, he may open your eyes.

Dick. Let me tell you, daddy, I'm as wide awake as you are.

William. I know you are, *physically*—but I allude to your mental sight. You are groping your way towards manhood, enveloped in a worse than Egyptian darkness, and——

Dick. [*Interrupting him.*] That'll do! I say, Pete, he talks like a minister, don't he?

Peter. That's a fact—and I shouldn't wonder if he was to be a parson one o' these days.

William. Your taunts, boys, will not divert me from the duty which I am endeavoring to perform, in persuading you to accompany me to our Sabbath-school. My time is limited, however, as I have to go and call for a young friend—but will be returning this way, when I hope you will have made up your minds to accept my invitation. (*Passes off.*]

Dick. I say, Pete—he's a droll chap, ain't he?

Peter. Yes, but I tell you what it is, Dick, he talks as though he meant it, don't he?

Dick. Yes he does. But pshaw! what's the use —a fellow might as well be dead, as to be going about with a long face, afeared all the time that he's goin' to do somethin' wrong. It'll do well enough for *men* to feel so, but boys *is* different. As for me I'm going to have as much sport as I can. Will you have a *smoker*? [*Takes off his hat and offers a cigar. They each take a cigar and smoke.*]

Peter. What do you call them?

Dick. Them's *real* Principes—" nothing else."

Peter. Real *Desperadoes*, more like. [*Puffs.*]— Jingo! they're strong enough to *take their own part*, any day.

Dick. Ye needn't smoke it, then—but I tell ye, they cost me three cents a-piece.

Peter. O what a choker! more like a cent a grab; ha! ha! ha!

Dick. [*Seizing him by the throat, and shaking him.*] Shut up, or I'll wallop ye like blazes:

[*Re-enter William hastily, followed by a girl. William approaches Peter and Dick and separates them, saying:*]

William. Come, come, boys—this will not answer. You ought to be ashamed of yourselves for conducting in such a manner on the Lord's holy Sabbath. I was in hopes of finding you in rather a different frame of mind. Have you considered the proposition I made you, about going to Sabbath-school with me?

Peter No we hain't—but I'll tell you what it is,

I've been thinkin' how it wouldn't hurt us to try it just for once, if we never went again. What do you say, Dick?

Dick. [*Who has been amusing himself by puffing smoke in the face of the girl.*] Say to what?

Peter. To going to Sabbath-school with Bill, here.

Dick. I can't go, no how; for I've got to sell all them papers, before I quit.

Julia. [*Stepping forward.*] My young friends, William has been telling me of his former interview with you, and I am glad to perceive that there is one of you willing to accept his kind invitation—and now there seems to be but one obstacle in the way of the other. Now, I have a proposition to make, and I know, William, that you, at least, will bear me out in it.

All. Why, what is it?

Julia. How much did these papers cost you, my boy?

Dick. [*Counting them.*] Just three shillings—and them "Messengers" ninepence: that makes three and ninepence. That's what they cost me.

Julia. Well, I propose that we raise that amount between us, to pay our young friend for the loss of his papers.

William. Agreed. [*Putting his hand in his pocket and counting out some change.*]

Peter. 'Nuff sed—though I hain't got a copper.

Dick. I'm willing, hand over the "*tin.*"

Julia. [*Taking out some money.*] I have only got two shillings—how much have you got, William?

William. I have only one; that will not be enough.

Dick. Never mind; I'll throw in the rest, and let it slide.

Julia. [*Handing him the money, and takes the papers, which she tears in pieces, and throws aside.*] There! I think that is the best way to dispose of them. Now, boys, hasten on to the Sabbath-school. [*Stepping forward to the front of the stage, while the boys make their exit.*] Now, my friends, you have seen a faithful picture of a class of the unfortunate youth of our city—unfortunate, I say, because they need parents or guardians to control them, and direct their footsteps in a "better way." They have been left to follow the inclinations of their own hearts, and "chose their own way." Perhaps many of those poor-looking, ragged little urchins, whose hoarse cries of papers for sale disturb the peace of our community each Sabbath morning, have had no kind friends to admonish them of the consequences of Sabbath-breaking, and lead them to the house of God on his holy day. Perhaps many of them are orphans, without father or mother to instruct them, or look after their welfare ; and being left to themselves, have fallen into company who love the pleasures of sin, and who will seek it though it cost the soul. Without moral restraint, and purchasers many for their sinful merchandize, with publishers more daring, if possible, than themselves, what can be expected of them but a total disregard of the Sabbath ? a total neglect of religious duty ? They are encouraged so to act, by finding men and women who want " the latest news," and will raise their windows and open their doors to receive the Sunday paper ; they will wait and watch, and as cheerfully pay for it as the boy receives their money. This is the root of the evil. Here, brother S——, is where the wrong lieth. This is the fountain from whence flows a current of sin and wickedness much more to be dreaded than the public imagines. If the reflection of Mr. Wesley, that " men buyers are exactly on a level with men stealers," is correct, may it not be said with as much propriety that the purchasers of Sunday papers are on a level with their venders ? Let the public refuse to buy them ; let Christians frown upon this desecration of the Lord's day, and these presses will stop, and these boys may be brought into the Sabbath-school and into the church. There is yet hope in their case. They can yet be saved. Many of these boys, an example of whose conduct and manners you have seen to-night, who spend their Sabbaths in playing ball and marbles, pitching pennies, selling papers, and cursing and swearing in our streets, are too often passed by in their wickedness without one word of warning from the professed followers of the Saviour. They give them no kind reproof; no Christian council; no salutary advice; but too often, like the Levite, pass on the other side. Oh! ye lovers of order and religion—ye who complain of the immorality of our youth, and say "such things ought not to be"—let your light shine and "go speak to that young man." There may be some among them, by the culture of now neglected minds, who may become statesmen and philanthropists, orators and ministers of the Gospel of Peace,—some Howards and Paynes, Wesleys and Whitfields, Hawkins and Goughs, whose influence in the cause of reform will be felt and acknowledged throughout Christendom. The Saviour came not to call "the righteous, but sinners to repentance." Oh, Christians!

let not one of these boys cross your path without your admonition and entreaty to forsake their evil way. Invite them with you to the house of prayer and to the Sabbath-school. "Cast your bread upon the waters and you shall find it after many days." They will not all forget your advice. It will follow them—in the still hours of the night, ere they close their eyes in sleep, some word you have spoken may awake the sleeping conscience, and bring them to repentance and to God. Try it, brother S——; try it, friends and patrons. "He which converteth the sinner from the error of his way shall save a soul from death, and hide a multitude of sins."

RECITATION.

INFANT SCHOLAR'S FIRST ADDRESS.

'Tis my grand debut on the stage,
    'Tis my first visit here—
I'm very little for my age,
    Just four years old this year.

If I should grow to be a man,
    I'll tell you what I'll do—
I'll try, the very best I can,
    To be as wise as you.

I'll learn to sing, and lead the choir,
    In Sabbath-school I'll teach—
And, should I catch the holy fire,
    Perhaps I'll learn to preach.

I don't intend to lie and swear,
    And break God's Sabbath day;
Tobacco must not go in *here*,
    Nor liquor go *this* way.

George Washington they call me home,
    I like that name, don't you?
It makes me think of fife and drum,
    The Red, the White, the Blue.

I guess you thought I couldn't speak,
    Perhaps you thought I'd cry—
You're much mistaken in your man,
    Hurrah for Fourth of July!

DIALOGUE.

BY A LITTLE BOY AND GIRL.

Stephen. Dear me, Frances, did you ever see such a crowd! Why, the people can't all get seats, that's certain. Oh! ain't it a pity our church is so small? Do look, Frances, even the galleries are full. I don't see where the folks all come from!

Frances. Come from, Stephen! They've come from home to be sure, to *see* us talk. It's a pity, I think, if they can't come once a year to see our school! I'm right glad to see them all. It shows they ain't quite forgot us, Stephen.

Stephen. No—no—they haven't forgot us. And ain't our superintendents tickled though! Such a crowd! Why, what a collection we'll have! I suppose they'll all give something. And what a library we'll have by and by! I guess we will. And then the boys and girls can all have a book.

Frances. Yes, and I'll have one too, Stephen.

Stephen. What do *you* want with a book, Frances? You can't read. You had better let the bigger girls have them.

Frances. I can't read, eh! Suppose I can't, mother can. And I've heard that the reading of Sabbath-school books convicted one mother, and she got converted. My mother will read them to me.

Stephen. Well, so she can, Frances. And I think maybe you can have one after to-night. We've got some real pretty books in our library, but not half enough. I wish the people would each give an extra sixpence to make it bigger, don't you, Frances?

Frances. No fears. I ain't afraid. There are so many of our friends here, that if they only hear we want books, will soon give Mr. B—— funds. Now let's both set down, like good children, and you'll see next Sunday if I ain't told you right.

Stephen. I don't doubt your word, Frances, for I

have heard father say the money market is getting better. But we'll wait and see. Good night, Frances.

Frances. Good night, Stephen.

HUMBLE, YET MIGHTY.

BY AN INFANT SCHOLAR.

" A little spring had lost its way
    Among the grass and fern ;
A passing stranger scooped a well
    Where weary man might turn.

He walled it in, and hung with care
    A ladle at its brink—
He thought not of the deed he did,
    But judged that toil might drink.

He passed again, and lo! the well,
    By summer never dried,
Had cooled ten thousand parching tongues,
    And saved a life beside."

DIALOGUE.

ORPHAN WILLIE.

BY THREE GIRLS.

Charlotte. (Seated, singing)

"Shed not a tear o'er your friend's early bier,
    When I am gone, I am gone;
Smile if the slow-tolling bell you should hear,
    When I am gone, I am gone;
Weep not for me when you stand round my grave,
Think who has died his beloved to save,
Think of the crown all the ransomed shall have,
    When I am gone, I am gone."

Sarah. I love that plaintive little song, dear Charlotte. It reminds me of our last Anniversary, when little Willie sang it on our Sunday-school platform. Don't you remember little Willie, who was only six years old, and yet spoke a long address and sung two pretty pieces? She attracted the audience with her musical voice, and spoke so plainly every body could hear her. She was dressed in pink, and looked so pure and modest—why don't you remember little Willie?

Charlotte. Yes, Sarah, I remember her sweet countenance and gentle manners very well. But that was a long while ago—she must be older now—why didn't our Superintendent get her to speak and sing this year, I wonder!

Sarah. Oh, Charlotte! don't you know the reason? She has gone where no tears are shed—where Jesus' own hand wipeth all tears from all eyes. She died the May following—and on her seventh birth-day. Around that sweet little girl (you know her proper name was Wilhelmina) much of hope was clustering—she made home cheerful and pleasant with her tuneful voice, her graceful step, and words of welcome. She possessed a good memory, and would commit and repeat many hymns and Scripture proofs, very correctly, when called upon. Besides, she was very sedate and gentle, and seemed always to prefer reading good books to playing like other girls. She was not mischievous or rude—but loving, quiet and studious. Why, Charlotte, I have been told that she never appeared elated or overjoyed except twice, when preparing to speak in Sunday-school—then her little heart seemed full of the spirit of the time, and she would be delighted to join the children in their holiday songs.

Charlotte. Were you, Sarah, acquainted with little Willie? I mean, do you know anything respecting her history, her brief life on earth? I have heard that she was left without her natural parents when a mere infant—that she was an adopted child. If you have time, will you not relate some incidents in regard to Willie?

Sarah. What little I have heard will not interest you, Charlotte. With your permission I will call in Emily. She can give you many facts that will be food for reflection, and have a tendency to make us thankful to God for all his gifts to us. I know a few things, but Emily can tell you best.

Charlotte. Do, please, call Emily. We can afford to spend a few minutes in reviewing the biography of that lovely child. I only saw her a few times, and thought I should love her very much. But I did not know she was dead. Yet, so it is,— "Death loves a shining mark," and its barbed quiver found one when it pierced the heart of dear little Willie. Some poet says:

> "I never loved a tree or flower,
> But 'twas the first to fade and die."

And many a Sunday-school can say its seats have been made vacant most frequently by the encroachments of Death among its lambs, " the loveliest and the best."

[*Enter Emily.*]

(Sarah rises and says,) Welcome, Emily! We were just wishing you were here, as you can tell something about Willie—" the observed of all observers" at our last Anniversary. Charlotte did not know she was dead till I told her just now, and expresses a wish to learn her history. Will you favor us with the narrative, Emily?

Emily. It would take too long, Sarah, to tell all. Let me just say that she was the only child of her mother, who was deserted to penury and want, by the man who vowed to be her husband for life at the marriage altar. When wedded about one year, after proving infidel to his vows, and spending time and substance in the haunts of intemperance, he left his home for California, without the knowledge or consent of his youthful, broken-hearted wife. To support herself and child, the mother found employ away from home, daily leaving Willie in charge of a grandmother *ninety-three years of age.* With a spirit too proud to have her circumstances known, she labored thus for two years, when she became the prey of consumption. No longer could she walk to her daily work—no longer could she earn her support. Good brother F—— and Dr. E. V. B——, and others visited her, and supplied her daily wants, and ministered to her spiritual necessities. Oh! such destitution, Charlotte! I cannot describe the scene. I have no comparison, for I have never seen its equal. Let me pass it over, and tell you how she died.

Charlotte. Please, Emily, tell me all. It stirs the heart in sympathy to hear about the poor. Bless me, how was it *possible* that the husband and father could leave in poverty *such* a wife and child! It is another instance, Sarah, of the effects of liquor!—the work of the "Demon of the Still." No doubt he loved the drunkard's drink before he was married. What a lesson to young, giddy-headed girls! Why, I'd rather live and die an old—— alone, I mean, than to be the companion of one who "tarrieth long at the wine." Shame on the man who calls himself a MAN, who will make the innocent suffer too for his want of principle! Who will yield himself—soul and body, wife and children—to the deadly influence of the drunkard's cups! But excuse me, Emily, I will not intrude my reflections longer. Tell us how she lived, and I won't interrupt you again.

Emily. Well, Charlotte, she was found, after entering a long alley, up a flight of rickety stairs, in a small room, carpetless, and comfortless. No furniture could be seen, except a table, a trunk beside it, two chairs, a small stove, the rocking-chair which held the aged grandmother and dear little Willie, and the cot on which the dying mother lay. If the room ever held more, I think they had been sacrificed to meet the landlord's claims. There, in one corner, emaciated and pale, we found a drunkard's wife—there lay the neglected one, whose glass had nearly run—a daughter of poverty. I knew her in her girlhood—when full of hope. I remember the glossy ringlets—the sparkling eye— the rosy lip she then possessed. And was this Henrietta? Was this the laughing, happy girl I knew eight years ago? Yes, it was poor Henrietta. The physician's skill was in vain—the night watchings of stranger friends availed not—the good old pastor's prayers were offered beside that cot for the last time—Death took no denial, and we put her in her shroud to sleep. Stranger friends gathered at the funeral ceremonies, and brought sweet white flowers to lay upon her breast. A few followed the remains to Union Cemetery—a few tears of sympathy found vent—and our good brother B—— lowered the coffin which contained Henrietta J——, the inebriate's wife—in the cold earth.

Sarah. Now tell us, sister Emily, of the Providence which directed the steps of the little orphan Willie.

Emily. Oh, yes—I love to think of Willie. Her poor mother, a few days before she died, gave her to a friend. After her wasted, trembling hand had made its signature mark, that "friend in need" took the little one to a better home. Willie had obtained another father, and another affectionate mother. By nursing and bathing and wholesome food, she grew up the beautiful child we saw her on the stage. Her school exercises were beside her foster-mother's knee—there she learned her alphabet—her arithmetic—her Scripture proofs —her many pleasant songs and recitations. She was one of the "olive plants" growing up around her new-found father's table—a cherished blossom, a tender flower on whom the winds seldom blew. "None knew her but to love her—none named her but to praise." Her little heart was full of affection, and although so young, she loved the ways of piety. We have heard her sing

> "I want to be an angel,
> And with the angels stand,
> A crown upon my forehead,
> A harp within my hand."

And I can imagine her, in the full fruition of the desire, amid the seraph throng with her crown and harp. Blest, departed one, "we'll all come soon."

Charlotte. Do you know, Emily, if her own father ever returned from California?

Emily. Yes, Charlotte, I understood that he came back after his wife had been dead about a year. He was seen drunk in the streets of New York—an outcast from respectable society. But "his sweet child and loving wife" he saw no more. To-night he fills a drunkard's grave. Lost! lost! And oh! Charlotte, when I think of the Judgment—that he will be there—that his short-lived wife, whom he vowed to love and cherish, will be there! What a scene! And Willie—sweet little Willie has gone to meet him there! What a meeting. Let the profligate hear it—let every drunkard hear it—"after death cometh the judgment." Oh! I hear the Judge saying, "Let him that is filthy be filthy still." "No drunkard hath eternal life abiding in him."

Sarah. Please tell us, Emily, was Willie long sick? And were you at her funeral?

Emily. Not very long—about six weeks. She took the scarlet fever—that uncertain, treacherous disease. We all thought she was getting well—but it suddenly assumed a dropsical type. One day she took up a newspaper, and reading its date, she said "twelve days more is my birthday"—but on that "twelfth day more" she took wings to heaven—the angels took her home on her seventh birthday, and released her spirit from the lovely, but delicate casket in which we saw her here. The Sabbath-school children bore the precious remains to the church—they wept when they remembered Willie—they saw her dressed as on the stage a few months before, now lying cold and lifeless before them. Some of them bent down and kissed the unconscious lips and marble brow. They had heard her sing, "I would not die in spring-time"—and her plaintive melody, "Shed not a tear o'er your friend's early bier"—and many were the heart-sobs of sorrow as brother H—— pronounced the solemn words, "Dust to dust, and ashes to ashes." The lonely, afflicted, suffering mother who had gone before her, gave good evidence of her pardon and acceptance with God, while lying upon her pallet of straw, and went to rest in the Christian's hope. Dear Willie, that sweet bud of promise, has also departed to be with Christ. We miss her glad voice in the Sabbath-school—we miss her at home. Our loss is Willie's gain. She has left our arms and our fostering care for the Saviour's fold. We'll leave her there—and, as the tears fall on memory's page, declare " *Good* what God gives— *just* what he takes away."

[*All rise.*]

EMILY.

A mound is in the grave-yard, a short and narrow bed,
The grass is growing on it, but no marble's at its head;
Ye may go and weep beside it, ye may kneel and kiss the sod,
But you'll find no balm for sorrow in the cold and silent clod.

SARAH.

Oh! think where rests your darling, not in her cradle bed,
Not in the distant grave-yard, with the still and mouldering dead;
But in the heavenly mansions upon the Saviour's breast,
With her mother's arms about her she takes her sainted rest.

CHARLOTTE.

She has put on robes of glory for the little robes ye wrought,
And she fingers golden harp-strings for the toys her sister bought;
Oh! weep, but with rejoicing, a heart-gem have ye given,
And behold its glorious setting in the diadem of heaven.

CHRISTMAS HYMN.

TUNE—"*There'll be no Sorrow There.*"

Once more we hail the day
  When JESUS came to earth—
Come, children! join our cheerful lay
  To celebrate His birth.

CHORUS.

To JESUS all praise belongs,
  To JESUS all praise be given—
Our ransom is paid—atonement is made,
  And Bethlehem's BABE is in heaven.

In glory still He lives
  Our ADVOCATE above—
Another Christmas day He gives,
  A token of His love.

Let youthful voices raise
  To GOD a grateful song—
Whose mercy lengthens out our days,
  Whose grace our years prolong.

Our chorus shall be praise—
    We'll bless MESSIAH's name;
Loud hallelujahs let us raise
    While angels do the same.

In flesh made manifest,
    The GODHEAD dwells below—
That INFANT on His mother's breast,
    Shall other gods o'erthrow.

Though in a manger born,
    He is the Father's SON!
And heaven and earth this Christmas morn
    Proclaim what He has done!

Dear SAVIOUR! meet us here!
    Once more young children bless—
With gratitude our hearts draw near
    To Thee, our RIGHTEOUSNESS.

All hail the sacred day!
    The WORLD'S REDEEMER hail!
Though brief on earth His mortal stay,
    He shall o'er earth prevail!

In triumph He ascends!
    The CONQU'RER of the Grave!
To come again, His faithful friends
    Forever more to save.

DIALOGUE.

BY A LITTLE BOY AND GIRL.

"MONEY WANTED."

Stephen. I am glad, Frances —— ——

Frances. Not one word, Stephen! Hold your tongue! You know what I told you on this stage last year, that unless we then got money enough, I was to speak first this time. And you know "as well as you live" that we didn't get money enough.

Stephen. That's true, Frances! You must excuse me—I really forgot. I guess we didn't get "money enough." But wasn't it heavy, though! I wonder how the Treasurer ever got home with all those black pennies! Didn't he get somebody to help him, Frances?

Frances. I don't know as to that, Stephen; but rather suppose his good little wife has had to darn his handkerchief for him. But why turn up your nose at "those black pennies," Stephen? Didn't every little fellow of them count one? And wasn't money *hard* then? "Pennies" were as "thick as hops," if my memory serves me, about this time last year. Hope you don't "despise the day of small things," Stephen!

Stephen. Not I, Frances! But don't people generally have things to *shine* about holiday times? I used to think so when I was a *boy!* Have the times *changed* lately, Frances?

Frances. Why, bless your heart, Stephen, don't you know they have? Time was, when Sabbath-schools didn't advertise for teachers,—and time was when they did—without getting them. Time was, when ministers came once every Sunday to talk with the children,—and time was when they didn't. Time was, when the silver was locked up in the banks, and a hard dollar was held as sacred as a faithful Sabbath-school Teacher—but the time is when they circulate freely.

Stephen. Pretty considerable of a change, Frances —I wonder what will occur next? Can you tell me, Frances?

Frances. I can't see into futurity, Stephen. I am no politician, as you may discover by my dress. Ladies generally attend to their domestic affairs, and leave such things to gentlemen. What do you know about it, Stephen?

Stephen. A nice way to find out my politics, Frances! Can't tell you, Frances. No place to talk on such subjects, at a Sabbath-school exhibition. I like to have things "all correct," Frances. But pray tell us if you know of any more changes, Frances.

Frances. I know what I should like, Stephen. I should like to see all the plates full of *change;* and above all things a little *change* in the number of teachers. I should like to see some of those young men, who smirk at the girls in the gallery, learning better manners in the Sabbath-school. I should like to see them behave as good as the children do when in the house of God, and not put so many bad pennies in the plate. Isn't that "all correct," Stephen?

Stephen. That's O. K., Frances; but who ever thought you would notice the young men? I guess you don't mind what the preacher says. Beside, if the ladies would look more at the pulpit, and less at the galleries, the young men would soon turn their eyes that way. Don't you think so, Frances?

Frances. No doubt of it, Stephen. And I hope to see some change soon. I think they had better stay home, than throw "sheep's eyes" in the church. It wasn't made to court in, was it, Stephen?

Stephen. No, Frances!—it is not at "all correct." But why change the subject of pennies to "sheep's eyes," Frances? I think we ought to retrace our steps, and get at the money matters again. We want money real bad, and there is no use of concealing it. How much do you expect to get to-night, Frances?

Frances. Quite a quantity, Stephen. Let's see—the gentlemen will give a dollar apiece—the ladies the same, OF COURSE. Do you know how many are here, Stephen? But we can't tell till we count the money. There are over five hundred, any how.

Stephen. And do you expect five hundred dollars, Frances?

Frances. Of course I do, Stephen!

Stephen. I don't believe it, Frances.

Frances. It is very ungentlemanlike and unscholarlike too, to doubt a lady's word, Stephen. You had better go home and get your manners, Stephen. Good night.

PIC-NIC MELODY.

WRITTEN FOR SOUTH SECOND-ST. SABBATH SCHOOL.

Tune—"*Wait for the Wagon.*"

On! come with me, my school-mates dear,
   To "Pleasant Valley's" shade—
Our Pic-nic comes "but once a year!"
   You need not be afraid!
Friend V———* takes the lead,
   And proffers us his care—
We've baskets full of goodly "feed,"
   And each shall have a share.
      Jump on the steamer,
      Hie to the steamer,
      Jump on the steamer,
         And we will soon be there!

Our B———r goes to help us sing—
   His happy face you'll see—
He'll make the very welkin ring
   When once he "gets the key."
"Dull Care" shall skulk away to-day,—
   To melody give place—
He shall not mar the children's play,
   Nor spoil one "pretty face."

* Insert Superintendent, Chorister and Librarian's names.

PIC-NIC MELODY.

  Three cheers for B———r,
  Long live our B———r,
  Three cheers for B———r,
   And three more for his choir!

For brother K———p one lengthen'd cheer
 Will wake the woodland sprites!
He's fairly earn'd new friends this year
 By " putting things to rights."
His " knowledge box" is running o'er,
 His thousand volumes tell—
We've felt his enterprise before,
 But we now feel " better as well."
   Bring out the banner
   Uplift the banner,
   Raise high our banner,
    And hurrah for the Grove!

Let laurels our Committee crown
 Who put our Pic-nic through,—
The good work has been " done up brown,"
 And many thanks are due.
We'll weave a garland for each guest,
 Who mingles in our feast—
Our Pastor too, among the rest,
 The last, but not the least.
   Swell, swell the chorus,
   Join in the chorus,
   Swell, swell the chorus,
    The last but not the least.

OPENING ADDRESS.

"GOD IS GOOD."

Delivered Celebration of Washington's Birthday, Feb. 22d, 1859, in the Mission Church,* Graham Avenue, Brooklyn.

BY A BOY.

CHRISTIANS AND FRIENDS OF THE SABBATH SCHOOL :

Will you permit a youth, like myself, to be the first speaker to-night? Will you condescend to listen, while I open the children's exercises on this two-fold Anniversary : the one hundred and twenty-seventh birthday of the "Father of his Country" and the celebration of our blessed Sabbath-school ? I take my appointed place on this platform to-night, feeling assured of my insufficiency to perform the task of pleasing, or even interesting such an audience—and therefore plead that 'the critic's dagger' may remain in its sheath, and hope you will not anticipate a tedious address, or much of originality in a short one.

---

*The first S. S. Anniversary in the new church edifice, on the site of the one just destroyed by fire.

I come first to say, that GOD IS GOOD—that he is the refuge of his people. In proof of this, my country lifts the arm of her power to-day; and the mountains and hills and valleys of her thirty-six United States reverberate the echoing voice—"God is good." The thousands of steeple-tops that point to heaven, throughout the length and breadth of our Christendom—the glorious, free institutions which America enjoys—our freedom to worship God as conscience dictates—our Christian Sabbaths—our peaceful firesides and happy homes—our Sabbath-schools in city and country, in town and village, in every nook and corner of our heaven-bestowed land,—*all* call for one joyous acclaim to-night, "God is good!" Could the Pilgrim Fathers, standing as once they stood on Plymouth Rock, exiles from oppression and superstition, be heard to-night —could they look over Columbia's vast territory— her cultivated fields—her millions of freemen—her thousands of cities and prairie homes—her shipping and navies—her modes of travel by land and ocean —could they, retrospecting the wilderness world in which they landed one century ago, look down upon us now, and witness the blessings of the free Republic which their wisdom and prowess planted, —I ask you, friends, would not each exclaim,

"What hath God wrought!" Could our Washington, after battling for the rights of Thirteen Colonies—after leading his victorious army through winters' storms and summers' heat—after witnessing the defeat of the enemy, and the retirement of British usurpation—after his hard-fought battles on victory-crowned fields—after his invocations and prayers that "God would make this land Immanuel's land"—now that the conquering hero has laid aside his armor, and retired to Vernon's shades and Vernon's grave,—I say could Washington be heard to-night, would he not point to those dark days of his earnest manhood, and say, "What hath God wrought!" Oh! ye people—ye who live in the light of this nineteenth century, and share the immunities of blood-bought freedom—ye who cherish the inestimable blessings of Peace, Equality, and Constitutional Liberty, join me in ascribing praise, and honor, and glory to the God of battles, and let every tongue proclaim "GOD IS GOOD."

For the sake of brevity, I leave these pleasurable thoughts of our country's prosperity, and turn me now to *ourselves*—to our plain, republican church—our unadorned sanctuary. My theme embraces much to cheer the hearts of the followers of Jesus, who worship in this humble temple—much to encourage them in their " labor of love " in winning souls to God. Well may *we* exclaim, " Hitherto hath the Lord helped us." Though few in numbers, and mayhap little in the eyes of the wealthier denominations, we claim to be "on the Lord's side." He hath watered this vine of His own planting; and we hear His voice to-night, speaking to His tried and faithful ones, " Arise, shine ; for thy light has come, and the glory of the Lord is risen upon thee." " For a small moment have I forsaken thee, but with great mercies have I gathered thee." Yes, it is but a brief period since we saw the flames feeding their fury upon our former edifice—since the burning element levelled to the ground the church we had dedicated, amid prayers and offerings, to the service of God. Then we took up Isaiah's lamentation—" Our holy and our beautiful house, where our fathers praised thee, is burnt up with fire : and all our pleasant things are laid waste." With hearts near to fainting, and sighs over the desolation which an inscrutable Providence permitted, we bowed in submission. "Fear not, little flock !" was sweetly whispered to the believing few ; and soon, the cinders and the rubbish removed, the mason's trowel and the carpenter's saw were heard like music to our ears. Praise to the benevolent-hearted—thanks to the contributors to the cause of Christianity in this isolated, missionary locality—honor to the unflinching spirits who stood like "the beaten anvil to the stroke"—but let us give all praise and thanks and honor, to Him who hath made us the people of his care, our "present help in time of trouble"—and let the mouth echo the sentiment of the heart : " God is good."

"By the grace of God we are what we are"— Methodist Protestants : protesting against Romish domination and priestly rule—against church and state organizations—against ecclesiastical aggressions—against anti-christian warfare upon the rights of the laity. We stand forth as a republican church, founded upon the great republican rock of Truth—the Bible. Upon our banner you may read, " whom the Lord maketh free, are free indeed ;" and it is our privilege to " Stand fast in the liberty wherewith Christ hath made us free, and be not entangled again with the yoke of bondage." We stretch forth our arms, and invite to our communion, the penitent, among the poor, the rich, the high, the low ; and we say to all, " Come with us " and " good shall come unto thee." Again are our walls erected ; again have we dedicated this sacred enclosure to God and " the things of the Spirit ;"

again our doors are open to receive "the returning prodigal"—those who have become bruised and mangled in the ways of sin—those who are devoid of peace—those who have been ensnared by the devices of the wicked one: come, we say, the ark of the Lord is open—escape for thy life—"Come and see that the Lord is good."

Let me not forget that one of the agencies of the Church to promote Scriptural holiness is our SABBATH-SCHOOL. This is the primary department—the drill-room for the young and inexperienced in the Christian warfare. This is our garden—*these* Teachers are the husbandmen—they prune the tender vines, and pluck out the tares, and water the growing plants every week, and we behold them flourishing and putting forth, and some are already bearing fruit to the glory of God. Many a wildflower has been transplanted and cultivated here—many an uncomely plant, which seemed to have been trodden under foot of men and little cared for, has been brought into our garden, tended and shielded from the storms, and to-night is blooming in beauty and promise, because its tendrils have taken root in good ground. Here are a few—behold them, friends! We do not expect to perfect them in the Sabbath-school. The Reaper will come by and by, as he has heretofore. The Lord of the harvest will himself transplant them—He will cull the good and leave the bad. And then, oh then, ye praying, faithful Teachers ! you will behold in "the new heavens and the new earth" that your "labor has not been in vain in the Lord." Scatter broadcast the seed, dear Teachers ! You know not which may yield—this or that, but withhold not your hand. Fill these little caskets with the precious truths of God. Give the children a knowledge of the Bible for their inheritance. Let them be fortified with this armor, and you may go down to your graves with the comforting assurance that your country is safe—that the church will have strong pillars and able supports—that Infidelity will retreat as the word of the Lord shall run and be glorified, even through your instrumentality. We cannot reward you, kind Teachers, for your patience and toil. Your reward is to come—it lies in the future. Wait—labor and wait. We may remain to bedew your graves with the tears of gratitude, and plant the willow of our sorrow beside your tombs—but *these* will not be your recompense. *Yonder* lies the victor's crown—*yonder* Jesus waits to place it on thy brow. And when the work is done—the end of care, the end of pain—

when you shall look back upon this land of ours—this little sanctuary—this blessed Sabbath-school—and see your works following you, I can now almost hear your hallelujah—" GOD IS GOOD."

CLOSING ADDRESS.

BY A BOY.

Before we part, dear friends!
   I'd like to say a word,
If you will condescend
   To let a child be heard.

I represent the claims
   Of all these little scholars,
And offer in their names,
   Our thanks for all your—dollars.

For them I here appear,
   With feelings of delight,
To wish you all a happy year,
   And bid you now—good night!

VALEDICTORY ADDRESS.

BY A BOY.

FOR CHRISTMAS ANNIVERSARY.

Stay, patient friends! a few words more
Before you hasten for the door—
Ere hat, and cane, and gloves you seek,
I have a few vague thoughts to speak.
I know you're weary—that is clear—
But "Christmas comes but once a year;"
And though our Sunday-school is *here*,
And you are living very near,
A long twelve months may pass away
   Before we see your face again—
So, friends, please listen to my "say"
The " Farewell Speech" for Christmas day,
   Which will not much contain.

You see by this, our Exhibition,
Our Sabbath-school's in good condition;
Since Brother C—— took supervision
Its "upper tendency" has shown
As youth to manhood fully grown.

Though small in statue, we can prove
He's quite a man in works of love:—
"He's gentle and he's kind" you know,
Which makes the children love him so.
In short, were he not standing near,
I'd tell what makes his name so dear.
Had I the power of nomination
I'd "have him up" to fill some station—
As Alderman—no, that's too low!
For Mayor I think he'd not *run* slow—
But higher yet is my intent,
A candidate for President!

One feature new has come to pass—
Our Preacher has a Bible-class,—
And every Sunday, rain or shine,
We have the help of our divine.
A good example for the Church
Whose members "leave us in the lurch"—
You take the hint, my worthy brother?
Then jog your friend—and *you* another.

I would of all our Teachers speak,
Though blushes might diffuse their cheek,
Whose faithful labors through the year
Have made them to us children dear.
But, ere I closed, it might be said,
"Do stop! it's time you were in bed."
So, I will let them pass review,
And "hurry up" and hasten through.

It has been whisper'd through the town
By Brother C—— and Sister B——n,
That a Melodeon we would get—
But really I ain't seen it yet:
'Twill be a blessing when we get it,
And I can tell you where to set it.
To those who would their aid contribute,
Who would their surplus funds distribute,
I now appeal—and we'll rejoice
With Music's elevating voice.
Please hand your dimes to any teacher,
Or you may trust them to the preacher.

Now, one word more, before adieu!
My Muse is tired, and so are you.
Come, Wednesday next, when we *repeat*,
And see these little urchins eat!
(Come early if you wish a seat.)
'Twill do you good. They take their **part**
As if they'd learn'd it all by heart—
Then, other exercises done,
They'll eager for the basement run;
All then are speakers—wide awake,
With open mouths for fruit and cake!

This treat our friendly Teachers give—
"To do the likes" long may they live.
Your "quarters" for admission here
Are meant to keep the School this year.

I'd like to see them! such a pile,
To make our honest Treasurer smile!
He'll keep 'em tight—and none will go
Unless the teachers vote him so.
Just one word more—my doggerel's done—
Our thanks to all our friends, each one.
Long may their presence grace the earth,
And infant voices speak their worth.

FOR THE BLANK LEAF OF A BIBLE.

Presented to a Sabbath School Scholar.

This, sister! is a priceless mine
    Of endless—sacred lore—
Here light and joy and love divine,
Like tendrils round the heart entwine—
    And life forever more.

To thee this Book—as pure as gold
    Refined—your Teachers give—
Deep in thy heart its truths enfold,
Its spirit there in meekness hold,
    While on the earth you live.

DIALOGUE.

BY A LITTLE BOY AND GIRL.

FINANCIAL.

Stephen. Well, Frances, are you on the stage again this year? Pray what have you got new to tell the people?

Frances. I declare, Stephen, if I wasn't better acquainted with you, I should think you meant to insult me. "Am *I* on the stage again?" And why not? I have tried to be a good girl, and don't think I have staid from school very often. There is nothing very new to tell, that I know of, only we are in great need of money.

S. The people won't think that's new, any how, for I never heard of a school in my life but wanted money. How do you know we want money, Frances, did the Superintendent say so?

F. Have you been a scholar so long, and yet don't know what we want with money? Fie! fie! Stephen—why, any of these little folks know as much as that! Suppose now I ask you a few questions. Don't we want wood to burn in the school this winter?

S. Of course we do, Frances—it's plaguy cold sometimes, even *with* wood.

F. Well, don't we want more books in our library?

S. Of course we do, Frances—for some of the books have been read over, and over, and over again—and as it now is, our librarian can't give us "things new and old"—besides, Frances, "variety is the spice of life."

F. Well, don't some of the children want shoes and clothes this inclement weather to come to school with?

S. Of course they do, Frances—"the poor we have always with us."

F. Well, ought not our school to give something, at least once a year, to the Sunday-school Union?

S. Of course it should, Frances—for I consider the Union as the parent society, and it becomes the duty of children sometimes to help their parents.

F. Well, then, Stephen, what made you ask what we wanted with money? I guess you only wanted to hold a dialogue with me, that our friends might hear the "why and wherefore." Perhaps you didn't want to tell yourself—but, remember, Stephen, that unless we get money enough to-night to prevent it, I'll try to speak first next time. Till then, be a good boy, Stephen.

S. Thank you, Frances. Good night.

FOR AN INFANT SCHOLAR.

(HOLDING A BIBLE.)

I want to be a preacher,
    And in the pulpit stand;
To point the way to heaven
    With the Bible in my hand.

I want to tell of Jesus,
    The Father's only Son—
His holy life—His painful death,
    And works which He has done.

I'd tell the suff'ring He endured
    For those He came to save—
How Love and Mercy filled his years
    And raised Him from the grave.

I'd give the world this Bible,
    The rich—the high—the low—
And teach the children early
    Its saving truths to know.

RECITATION.

ON THE DEATH OF A TEACHER.

BY A BOY OR GIRL.

"Green be the turf above thee,
    Friend of my early days;
None knew thee but to love thee,
    None named thee but to praise."

            Thy will be done,
Our Father and our God. The time is come!
The silver thread is broken! and we weep
For one, now cold and lifeless, who was here,
In manhood's strength, engaged for Heaven,
With heart and hand—a noble "doer of the work."
Ay, it is finished!—it is early done!
The summer flowers have just been nipped,—
Their fragrant sweets just vanished, and the leaves,
Seared by the chill of Fall, no longer green,
Lay scattered round, and wander with the breeze;
The birds have fled—their music, too, is gone,—
And sighing winds, like to a requiem dirge,
With us now seem to mourn the fate of man,
And whisper that loved name—our Teacher.
We have borne him hence. No more he meets us here,
As erst in that familiar way he used,

Faithful to perform the task his Saviour blest,
And cheered him on his course. Consigned to dust,
A sleeper in the chambers of the dead,
His voice we hear not.—'Tis with us no more
First in the choir of infant praise, where meet
The bright-eyed, tender forms, who, once his care,
Look yet to find their friend—but ah! in vain.
He is not here, save 'mid the seraph throng,
Celestial spirits who have winged their flight
From Heaven's throne, bright witnesses on earth
Of this our offering.
           But hark! there comes
A still small voice, divine and gracious,
To the ear of Faith, a cordial for our loss :—
"He is not dead, but sleepeth." Spring may come,
The trees may blossom, and the rose may bud,
All nature wake to harmony and joy:
Yet he will not be here, to drink the dew,
The early droppings, or with gladdened heart
Give thanks. Nay! Eden is his home, more blest,
Nor change nor death affects the dweller there,
And summer is eternal, fresh and fair.

  We come, pale sleeper! with the wheels of time
To journey on, ere long to meet thee; yea,
Perchance, as sudden as thine own decease,
In bloom of life, to change this mortal state,
And find a place of rest with thee, above,
In Him who says to all, "Come unto me."

DIALOGUE.

ON THE DEATH OF A FEMALE SUPERINTENDENT.

BY FIVE GIRLS.

Mary. "Happy New-Year," Sarah. I am glad to meet you again in the land of the living, under such favorable circumstances. We have passed through another year; and while death has taken away many cherished friends, and silenced on earth many voices we loved to hear, the Lord has been very kind in sparing our lives.

Sarah. Yes, indeed, Mary, "the Lord has been very kind." Yet you seem in a more solemn mood than usual. I should expect you to be more lively to-night than any other. This is New-Year's evening, child—and people should be cheerful on the first day of the year, I think.

Mary. True, Sarah, "but there is a time for all things." And no doubt I should have felt as happy and 'cheerful' as you now do, had I not, in looking round among our beloved Teachers, missed one of the number who was wont to be foremost and busiest in our exhibitions. If you will just cast your eyes over the assembly, and think for a moment—'*are our teachers all here?*' you will no doubt miss the one I do.

Sarah. (*after a pause*)—Well, Mary, I have been looking—but it's difficult to miss *one* in such a crowd. It is to me, like missing a star when the sky is thickly set with them. But, perhaps, Mary, it was one you loved very much, or loved the most —and not finding her here as usual, you miss her company more than any other. Perhaps it was your sister, or your mother, who were here last year, and you have since buried them.

Mary. Oh! no, Sarah—I must say again 'the Lord has been very good'—and neither my sister or mother are missing—they are both here—but one is not here who took so much pleasure with the children—whose eyes would sparkle with delight when she saw the infants here climbing to their seats, or heard their mellow voices singing some pretty little air—or when some little girl or boy would be speaking their piece, how she would smile in approval, and take them down from the stage with a kiss for pay! Ah, yes! I can now see her in my mind, gently leading a little girl to the steps and helping her up, to recite the verses on little Anna Gray. How little we thought that 'where Anna was gone' she so soon would go! I mean, Sarah, our female Superintendent, my dear friend and teacher—whose counsels were given with such warmth of feeling in behalf of her scholars. Have you not missed her this evening, Sarah?

Sarah. Being New-Year's, Mary, when all is life and merriment, I had not thought of her till now—and it's strange I did not, for I loved her very much. She was one of our earliest and most faithful teachers. I was a member of her class in Sabbath-school, and many have been the happy hours I used to spend with her.

Eliza. I am sorry to interrupt your conversation, girls; but as I heard Mary mention the name of our Superintendent, I thought I would ask her why she is not here to join in our anniversary as usual.

Mary. Oh! Eliza, she is in a much happier place than this. She will no more join us in our exhibitions, or congratulate us on the return of New-Year's day, but is now celebrating the praises of God where New-Year's never ends. Mrs. V—— H—— is dead, Eliza, and is no longer suffering in the flesh—she is no longer an inhabitant of the earth, but a dweller in eternity—among "the ransomed and redeemed of the Lord."

Emma. (a very little girl)—Has she gone to stay, Sarah? Ain't she coming back again, never?

Sarah. She has gone to stay, dear Emma. She will not come to us, but we may go to her. She used while here to point us to the place where she has now gone. Can you tell me where it is, Emma?

Emma. Why, she is close by me, Sarah. Didn't our teachers put her in the grave-yard behind the church?

Sarah. Yes, my little one, they buried her body in the church-yard; but that body we loved so much was only the house in which Mrs. V—— H—— lived. The house has fallen to decay—it is crumbling back to dust; but its tenant—the soul—the thinking part—the spirit—has fled from earth to heaven. Yonder, Emma, far above the "twinkling stars," our dear teacher is to-night living. Mary said "Mrs. V—— H—— was dead"—but I say no—she is living. Our minister says the good shall live forever; don't they, dear Pastor?

Emma. Well, I am sure our Superintendent was good. She used to come to our Infant School, and was always so kind and clever. I wish she could come back again. But if she ain't dead, Mary, how did she get up into heaven above the twinkling stars?

Mary. The 'angels of God' came for her, Emma. They were in the room where she died, and clapping their bright wings bore her away to be forever with the Lord.

> "Hark! they whisper—angels say,
> Sister spirit! come away."

Her tears are all dried now, Emma—her sighing is all at an end. She will no more visit your Infant Class, to encourage *these* little ones to be good, or take them in her arms and soothe them when they cry. She has fallen in her usefulness—in the midst of her years, and left her companions behind. But she has fallen asleep:

> "Asleep in Jesus!—Time nor space
> Debars this precious 'hiding place'—
> On India's plains, or Lapland snows,
> Believers find the same repose.
> Asleep in Jesus? Oh, for me
> May such a blissful refuge be."

Sarah. Perhaps, Mary, you can tell us something of her history, and of her death-bed scenes. I think it would interest the children to hear something of her experience. Did you call and see her while sick? She was confined to her room a good while, I believe. Her place has long been vacated in the choir where she used to sit.

Mary. I cannot tell, Sarah, so much about her as Frances can. She has been longest in the Sabbath-school, and better acquainted with her history, perhaps, than I am. Will you be kind enough, Frances, to give Sarah the information she asks of me?

Frances. Good evening, girls. I have been listening attentively to your conversation—the more so, because the subject of it was one who was dear to my heart. The name of Mrs. V—— H—— is sweet to my ear—and touches a chord that vibrates at the sound. I can say with Sarah that "I loved her very much." Oh! yes, we all loved her very much, but God loved her better, and has taken her from among us.

> But though her shade has left the earth,
> And sought its native sphere,
> Her name, by those who knew her worth,
> Shall long be cherished here.

I know but little of her history, Mary; but this I know, she was "faithful unto death." She was brought into the fold of Christ when only sixteen years of age, and I am told was never known to leave the "object of her love," or turn aside from the pursuit of "the crown which lay at the end of the race." In proof of this, I appeal to the leader and members of her class, if there are any here.— Ah! yes, I see many. The tear of affection is starting from the eyes of some. Sisters! do you remember your now sainted companion? Do you remember how she told you of her hopes and desires—of her joys and her sorrows—of her fellowship with God, and her consolations in believing? Do you remember her kindly ways, and how her heart was knit to yours—how she would "weep with those who wept, and rejoice with those who rejoiced"—how faithfully she toiled with you at the mourners' bench, and how her soul was glad when one and another gave God their hearts? Do you remember her in the tented grove? Do you remember her in the family circle—what kindness ran through all her acts? Do you remember her in the singers' seat, ye who are left behind? Ah! yes. She is no longer there—her voice is hushed, and her fingers will no more turn the leaves to find a tune. Her song of praise is now more sweet— she worships near the throne.

'She hath grappled and triumph'd o'er death,
  And rush'd through his caverns of gloom—
She hath drawn the unquenchable breath,
  In beauty immortal to bloom.
She hath stretched forth her gossamer wings
  O'er the azure of boundless repose—
And drank of the nectarine springs,
  Where the river of Paradise flows.'

She joined this society long before this church was erected. Her time—her prayers—and her contributions she gave for Zion here. Here were the people of her choice. Here, while in health, she could be found, whether the church was in prosperity or adversity—in sunshine or in clouds. But she was taken sick. Soon after our last exhibition she became the prey of disease—her body wasting under the consumption for several months, when she fell asleep in the Saviour.

* * * * * I cannot describe that death-bed scene, Mary. I cannot tell it. But if you wish to know whether she was willing to die, I can tell you, Yes—anxious—desirous to "depart and be with Christ." Her treasure had long been in heaven, and there was her heart also. She daily expected her change to come, and often inquired of her friends if they thought she could last much longer. No murmurings escaped her lips. God was just; and though emaciated with disease, and greatly afflicted, she bore it with confidence that she was going home to her Father's house, to go no more out forever. And there, children, amid that blood-washed throng, she has met some of our school-mates, our brothers and sisters, parents and friends. There she has met brothers H———, and P———, and S———. There she has met sisters B——— and M———. There she has met little Johnny, and Hannah, and Anna, and those who loved and were beloved of her, while dwelling on the earth. From heaven she is calling upon us all to be faithful—to improve our time, and use well our privileges. On one here her "mantle has fallen." And who is she so honored? To that one she is calling. To our newly-elected Superintendent her walk, her conversation, and her diligence in this her former field of usefulness is to-night kindly speaking, and do not speak in vain. To ministers and people, and especially to our teachers she is speaking: "Work while the day lasts, for the night cometh wherein no man can work." To my school-mates the prayers and tears of our dear departed Teacher are loudly appealing. Yes, children, she has prayed with you for the last time. She has spent the last

Sabbath with us. That familiar form and voice are seen and heard no longer. We have lost a steadfast friend. This Church has lost a strong pillar. One of her bright lights has gone out here to shine above. While we are singing here she is singing in glory—and if we prove faithful to God will no doubt welcome us there when we also come to die. I expect to see her again, Eliza. I expect to hail her disembodied spirit by and by in Paradise. I expect in the resurrection morning, when the earth and the sea shall give up their dead, to strike hands again with Catharine. With this hope we closed her eyes in death, and left her in the tomb. With this hope let us bear our loss with composure, and gladly wait the hour. Farewell, beloved!—" Though lost to sight, to memory dear." Farewell! farewell!

> We'll meet again in glory,
>   Our joyful notes to raise—
> To shout redemption's story,
>   In never-ceasing praise.

NEW-YEAR'S ADDRESS.

BY A GIRL.

Dear Friends and Patrons! since 'tis mine to greet
Such cheerful faces as my gazes meet,
I gladly bid you now a welcome here,
And wish you all a truly Happy Year.

Yes, Time has sped his race on rapid wings,
And claims the tribute which the Old Year brings;
Its cares and joys, its toils and pleasures, too,
Are his forever!—none dispute his due,

The flight of Time!—what meditative thoughts
Should it awaken, as we note his course—
How oft the past to ponder, and to learn
The little while our "lamp of life" will burn!

And what the record of the year that's gone?
Have we no mis-spent time to vainly mourn?
Or have our hours in cheerful duties sped,
While blessings have been showered on our head?

With joyful hearts we praise that bounteous hand,
Which still enriches and preserves our land—
With gratitude our souls shall long be full,
And may we feel it for our Sabbath-school.

That happy place, where children first are taught
To shun all vice and every evil thought;
And in their youth to trust and serve the Lord—
To keep his precepts and to learn his Word.

And oh! the joy to mingle with that throng,
And share the pleasure of their happy song—
To dwell in peace, and learn our Teacher's will,
A Sabbath-scholar sure alone can feel.

And then the hours—how sweetly do they glide,
In learning pleasant lessons side by side;
Each one to help the other, and to make
The path to Knowledge easy as 'tis great—

To take our playmates from the noisy streets,
And safely lead them to our school-room seats,
'Till they return no more to vicious ways,
But give to Jesus their remaining days.

But why should I presume to picture forth
The blessings of our School, or Teacher's worth;
Their claims to patronage you all must know—
Abundant smiles approving, tell me so!

I therefore now must bid a brief farewell
To this kind audience, whom I wish to tell,
That others who are waiting, have to say
Some little things appropriate to the day.

So then, kind friends, as thus I've "broke the ice,"
I'll take my leave, and usher in a trice,
Some smart young scholars, who, I rather guess,
Will please you better than this short Address.   T.

LINES

Written in a Bible presented to a Teacher on leaving his Class.

Dear brother beloved! 'mid thy perils abroad,
Let thy heart be still firm in the Word of the Lord;
Let thy faith never fail thee—thy hope never dim,
But with courage unshaken rely upon Him.

When o'er the bleak mountains—across the blue main,
We'll pray for thee, brother—to meet thee again;
If not in our Sabbath-school, may it be given
To meet thee at last in the "kingdom of heaven."

CHRISTMAS ADDRESS.

BY A BOY.

Dear Friends, Officers, Teachers, and Fellow-Schoolmates—We are met to-night, after the lapse of another year, to celebrate the glad anniversary of the birth of Christ, our Saviour.

Eighteen centuries ago, the gates of heaven opened, and as the light of an immortal day streamed forth on our sin-darkened world, angel voices heralded in exultant, joyful song, the advent of the Holy One—our blessed Redeemer. The light that then first bathed the earth with its infant ray, bringing the promise of life and health to the nations, is fast mounting to its zenith. We have beheld its almost noontide splendor, have felt its warmth and life-giving power, and now may well with reverence vail our eyes in holy adoration before the Sun of Righteousness. It is certainly fitting that a day thus consecrated should be becomingly remembered. If then ushered amid the loud hallelujahs of cherubic song, breathing hope and promise, surely we who inherit its blessings, should with glad and grateful hearts, waft our praises to that throne where Bethlehem's babe, now risen in triumph, ever liveth to make intercession for us.

Three years have passed since last we met, and what great changes have they brought to us and to our nation! How many who were then with us, to-night we look for in vain! And ah! where are they? True, some have removed to other fields of labor in the Sabbath-school work. Some from our school have gone to battle for our Country's rights —teachers and scholars. With hearts and minds quickened by the influences of our blessed religion, as here thrown around them in days of uninterrupted prosperity and peace, they presented their bodies a living sacrifice on the altars of Patriotism none the less willingly because previously consecrated on the altars of Piety. Bravely have they fought, and some have nobly died to vindicate the Right. While we are here, radiant with life and health, amid festivity and gay rejoicing, we still may sigh in sympathy and sorrow with the friends who here so deeply mourn the forms of loved and lost, present and happy with us at our last anniversary, but to-night chill and lonely as they rest in Southern graves. Some have returned again, spared through many a hard-fought battle. With heart-felt gratitude and pride, we welcome them to our school once more. They went at the call for volunteers, and bravely and patiently endured the consequent toil and suffering. God bless and reward them!

Thanks to the kind interest and prayers of you, our Teachers, many of us, under the blessing of God, have sought and found the Saviour; and this church to-night holds hearts throbbing with the new-born joy, faces aglow with peace toward God and man, to whom these walls and scenes are endeared by ties and associations only known and appreciated by those who have had a like blessed experience. To many a young pilgrim here it has proved a very Castle Beautiful, where, cheered by Piety, Prudence and Charity, and girded with a Christian's sword and breast-plate, he has been enabled to contend against the darts of the persecuting Apollyon. Yes, grateful young hearts may ever say, "If I forget thee, O Jerusalem! let my right hand forget her cunning. If I do not remember thee, let my tongue cleave to the roof of my mouth; if I prefer not Jerusalem above my chief joy."

Some have been summoned from our school to taste thus early the higher, holier joys of heaven; have passed peacefully from our sorrowing world, leaving to us so many clear and cheerful evidences of their Christian triumph. But while our school has been thus affected by removal, death and marriage, it has steadily increased until the present time, and now outnumbers any previous year. I am told by our Superintendent, that we are much in want of teachers—faithful, pious teachers, who love this blessed work of saving souls. Friends, look at the field, the fruit of which you are called to gather in. It is whitening for the bright harvest day. Then come, thrust in the sickle, gather your sheaves, and place them in the garner of the Lord.

And now look around you, friends, and tell me, does there not seem to be a peculiar appropriateness in the joy of childhood on such an occasion as this? Indeed may we not almost claim the day as our own? Christened by the sweet smile of the infant Jesus, it has been a happy holiday for the young ever since, to be endeared to us more and more each succeeding age, as the plan of salvation has been more fully unrolled, and the attendant blessings of civilization—with peace on earth and good will to man—multiplied and more generally made known. Think you that we forget that Jesus was once a child ? No ; rather were infancy and childhood sanctified and made more blessed by his advent. Responsive to its blythe buoyancy and irrepressible gladness ; sympathizing with its peculiar temptations and sorrows ; obedient to its duties and patient of its restraints, the Lamb of God cherished the same love for Joseph and Mary that now brims our hearts, as to-night we thank God for a Christian father and mother, and the sweet influence of "Home, sweet home." Yes, we see those extended arms of blessed invitation, and our hearts yet bound with joy as we hear the tender reproof—oft repeated, yet never growing old— "Let the little ones come unto me and forbid them not, for of such is the kingdom of heaven." Nor do we forget the yearnings of youthful aspiration and pious responsibility which prompted the, "Wist ye not that I should be about my Master's business ?" And to-night these smiling faces and joy-lit eyes, tell of the happiness we feel in being participants in the universal good—though little, yet "workers together with God."

Then we proudly welcome you, friends and teachers—all, while with hymns of praise and our best endeavor, we cheerily celebrate our Christmas Jubilee. JR.

RECITATION.

BY A BOY.

A MESSAGE TO CHRISTIANS.

Kind friends and patrons! who come here
To see our School from year to year,
I have a message, short and true,
That I must now repeat to you.

Here you will find, each Sabbath day,
Some ill-bred children out at play,
Whose parents, wanting in control,
Use not the means to save the soul;
But let them loose, without a guide,
To curse and swear, and God deride—
To break His laws, His ways to shun,
And eager after death to run.
Oh! were they taken by the hand,
And brought where youthful minds expand,
How better far their hearts might grow,
And credit to their names bestow!
Come, bring them, friends! we want to see
Our room filled up—'tis large and free:

Our School-room, loved and honored place,
Where we may meet them face to face.

Now is the time—ere they begin
To tread the darkened paths of sin—
Ere lost to Virtue—lost to Truth,
Lost in the days of early youth,
Oh, Christian! let thy Lord's commands
Live in thy heart, and move thy hands—
Rise! seek them out, and let them share
The blessings of this house of prayer;
Where God displays his matchless grace,
And welcomes all who seek His face.
Here they will find that "solace strong"
Which to the wicked ne'er belong—
Here they may come, when sorely tried,
And learn that Christ for them hath died:
To this blest spot direct their feet,
And lead them to the Mercy-seat.

Give to our youth the proper bent,
And let their time be better spent
Than mocking God with idle play
Upon the Christian's Sabbath day:
Than pitching pennies—flying kite—
Than engine running—out at night—
Than circus going—smoking—fighting—
In the road to hell delighting:
Teach them to shun the drunkard's fate,
And learn his doom before too late:

Let them in Wisdom's ways be taught,
And to our Sabbath-school be brought.
Then, then, ere long sad crime would cease,
And prison-members would decrease;
And children find their sins forgiven,
And love the path that leads to heaven.

TRIBUTE

ON THE DEATH OF A SCHOLAR.

BY A GIRL.

MR. SUPERINTENDENT:—I listened attentively to the language used by my friend in the opening address.— He mentioned the names of dear ones " on the battle field" who were attached to our Sabbath-school—he said " the spoiler has been here," and pronounced the familiar names of [two] of our Teachers whom " the hearse had removed from our sight"—but the name of [Priscilla,] one of our most cherished scholars, I did not hear. And why did I expect to hear it? Because she too has passed away from earth—from this School of her love and her youthful days—from these companions of her happy childhood. She expected to join us in our Sabbath-school festivities—she anticipated taking part in these exercises to-night as she had formerly done; but just as the glad new-year opened with hope for us all, "the spoiler came" and nipped our sweet bud of promise. It has withered at his touch, and is gone! She is not here; and I do not wonder that many who knew her feel sad and lonely to-night, even amid the hilarity of our returning anniversary. I know comparatively little of her short life's experiences: but this I know, [Priscilla] was a good girl—a constant attendant of the Sabbath-school, and I have no doubt our sister and friend has gone to the heavenly world to dwell with the saints in light. Yet the separation is afflictive—the hours of innocence and joy we have spent together—now gone, forever gone—makes me feel sorrowful, and I cannot help it. We used to come to church together, in winter and in summer time, and join in the same hymns of praise and thanksgiving. To-night, how changed the scene! I come to my Sabbath-school, and look in vain among the happy group—[Priscilla] is not there. I am here on the earth, enjoying the pleasures and friendships of my childhood yet, while she is sleeping beneath the earth—a tenant of the grave! Oh, call me not weak—chide not the gushings of sympathy over the memory of my departed friend, nor the falling tear, when a scene like this recalls her to my heart.

The Lord hath called her early from the ills and disappointments of the present life, and taken her to himself. The companions of her earthly state may weep over her early fall, and sigh when her name is spoken —but it cannot replace her—they cannot call her back ! One of your " household flowers" has been transplanted to a more genial clime. She heeds not the wintry blast. The keen winds may sweep over her mortal resting place, and chant her requiem through the weeping willows—but they harm her not. "The spirit goes to God"—and there, after a little while, you and I will be called to stand, to be judged for all we do. No partings come in heaven. The friends we cherish here may be called to pass through years of suffering, and waste away by the slow-consuming fires of disease—but there is a world where death hath no power—where there is no sickness or sorrow—and friends long lost on earth are friends again in heaven. [Priscilla] has left us ; but by and by we shall be reunited in immortal youth. The eye once sparkling and bright is closed—the voice so tuneful in the Sabbath-school is hushed. It is a warning to us, dear schoolmates, that we are not too young to die ! I little thought, at our last Anniversary, when [Priscilla] stood here, that she would die before another such meeting. And little did she think, when dressing for that exhibition, she would to-night be dressed in the drapery of the tomb! I little thought when she was singing here of "the happy land, far, far away," that she would reach it so soon. But, so it is. She has left here her little circle of warm-hearted friends—the children of her Sabbath-school are here—her affectionate Teacher is here—her Pastor is here—her Superintendent is here—but she has escaped away! In yonder world of "spirits bright" she has found new companions—new glories spread before her—and the glad song of souls redeemed there chime in her welcome home. I leave her there. God grant we may all meet her there. The passport to that happy home is "Holiness, without which no man shall see the Lord." If you and I, therefore, would see our deceased friend again, we must be holy. The holy Apostles and martyrs and saints of the olden time will be there—and the blessed Saviour, who has ransomed us with his own precious blood, will be there. Let us remember, friends,

> "Nothing is worth a thought beneath
> But how we may escape the death
>   That never—never dies;
> How make our own salvation sure,
> And when we fail on earth, secure
>   A mansion in the skies."

HYMN OF PRAISE.

Now let our joyous hymn of praise
    To Jesus' name ascend,—
Come, children! give these happy days
    To Christ, the children's Friend.
Chorus—Then let us all rejoice and sing,
    And make our School with music ring;
    God will accept the offering—
        The children's song of praise.

Dear Saviour! from thy mercy-seat
    Look down on us to-day—
Direct our little wandering feet
    In Wisdom's peaceful way.

Father! our Sabbath-School inspire
    With Faith, and Hope, and Zeal;
Give to each heart the sacred fire,
    And Thy adopting seal.

Our noble youth are gathered here
    To learn the Law Divine,—
Kind Teacher! may its light appear,
    And on our pathway shine.

In God we will exult and sing
    Till we obtain the prize,—
And praises, which the children bring,
    Shall like sweet incense rise.

DIALOGUE.

On the Introduction of Gas-light into the Church.

BY A BOY AND A GIRL.

Boy—Come here, little sister! I've something to say
On the "march of improvement" we see in our day—
I mean in the Church where our Sabbath-school meets,
Our dearly-loved Church—the Church with "free seats."

Girl—I'll listen, dear brother! a moment or two,
For I'm always delighted with things that are new:
'Tis a prosperous omen—but do not forget,
In getting new things we should not get in debt.
But where shall I look? or where shall I go?
The "improvement" you speak of don't make a great show.

Boy—And do you not see? Why, where are your eyes?
Such a beautiful light! and can't find the prize!
Look about you, dear sister! pray, don't be afraid,
Your eyes to "see wonders" the Lord himself made.

Girl—I see the Church crowded—that's not what you mean,
For often before the same thing I have seen,—

I see smiling faces, with hearts full of cheer,
Who come to our Church at least once in the year—
Provided our School should a festival give,
You'll find them all present " as sure as you live."
I saw a great basket, with cakes running o'er—
Not these that you mean, for we've had such before.
I see some new scholars—some Teachers, I ween,
Who fill up the places of others I've seen—
Of some who've departed, as year follows year,
Of others who married—and they are not here!
I see Mr. B———, with signs of contrition
For voting against our School Exhibition—
I see our kind Pastor, " a Sabbath-school man,"
Who visits the children " as oft as he can."
I see the Committee of Twelve, I declare,
Who promised to aid in our meetings for prayer!
But these are not *new*—they're familiar to all,
The old and the young, the great and the small.

Boy—Well, sister! indeed your perception is clear,
But are there no objects of interest yet near,
Which gladden your eyes, and fill with delight
Our Sabbath-school patrons and friends here to-night?
Pray, don't you perceive—I think you well may—
That the old Doric lamps have been taken away?
And now in their stead (just " ope your discerners")
Behold the bright rays from our new-fashioned burners!
A short time ago, and the light was so dim
That our Dominie Patient could scarce read his hymn—

In searching the words the choir lost the tune,
For really 'twas worse than " the light of the moon":
So gloomy—so doleful—each face here appeared
That a very " green child" could be easily " sccered."
'Twas something like this that your eyes now discern*—
So, feeble and faint the old lamps used to burn!
But a noble committee, the best in the town,
Consisting of gentlemen Johnson and Brown,
Conceived the wise plan, and brought it to pass,
Of lighting our neat little chapel with Gas.
They asked of their friends (excusing us scholars)
To aid in the cost—about two hundred dollars,
Which soon was subscribed—but ain't it a sin,
A good many pledges have not been paid in!
I was glad from my heart when the work was begun,
And " twice was I glad" when I saw it all done :
No longer, thinks I, will the Sexton complain
And *turn* up his nose with perfect disdain
As he trimmed the old lamps; but, *turning* a screw,
He'll do his work better, and much cheaper too.
I go for the Gas, 'tis so pleasant and clear,
And hope we may all have a brighter New-Year.

---

* The sexton at this point will turn down the gas, so as to leave a dim light like that of the lamps—and, after a brief pause, turn the gas on again.

DIALOGUE.

ON THE DEATH OF A PIOUS SCHOLAR.

BY TWO BOYS AND ONE GIRL.

Alfred. Ah! and how is brother Reuben to-night? I am happy in joining with you in the pleasing exercises of our Exhibition again, and trust we shall have a delightful time. But, pray tell us, brother Reuben, what makes you look so melancholy? I had expected to see my young school-fellows all mirth and pleasure on this occasion, any how. You are not well, perhaps.

Reuben. O yes, I am very well, Alfred. But you must allow me to differ in opinion respecting "mirth and pleasure" in the house of God. I see too much of it every Sunday among some of the young men and ladies in our church—and for my part, I think it is shameful. Besides, Alfred, the return of our Anniversary touches the chords of memory, and "other days come back" in all their sweetness—days and years when our Sabbath-school was enjoying more favor, and when more interest was taken in these——

Alfred. Pardon my interruption, brother Reuben. I have long felt anxious to know why such a falling off of interest by the church. I have noticed at children's baptisms a strong desire that the infant may be brought up in the "fear and admonition of the Lord"—and yet the Sabbath-school, the best place in the world to train them for God and usefulness, how much it is neglected! It seems to me, also, we have fewer children here than at our former exhibitions. And some, I remember, who took part with us on the stage. Where are they?

Reuben. Some there are, I believe, who think they have grown too big for Sabbath scholars; some are absent for a time; and there was one, who has left us, never—no, never to return. Perhaps you know, brother Alfred, who I mean. Don't you remember the little boy who spoke so nobly last year—and who "wished he was a man to fire his cannon too?"

Alfred. Remember him! I guess I do. We were members of the same class—at the same altar we have often knelt—from the same book we used to sing praises to Jehovah—and to the same teacher have our Scripture proofs been recited. Truly, I loved him, Reuben, and I think he was beloved by all our teachers. And as the poet justly says, "He never loved a tree or flower, but 'twas the first to fade and die"—so I find it as I grow up in life. But here is Eliza, whose companion he was for two successive years in this very place. Maybe she can tell us something interesting about "the loved and lost."

Eliza. I think you refer to little Johnny, do you not, Alfred? (Assent.) Certainly, I remember the last time he was at school. It was in March last. He was not well enough then to be out, but he loved his school, and begged his mother to let him come. I can almost see him now, in his little frock coat and cloth cap, hand in hand with his sisters, hastening in the cold or wet to the place he loved so well. But he has left us, as our brother Reuben said, never—no, never to return. He is an angel now—and I don't know but he is one among the cloud of witnesses of which St. Paul tells us—I don't know but he is permitted to look down upon this the place of his second birth to-night. Yes, I have thought I could see him amid the "multitude which no man can number." Excuse these feelings, my brother, think it not weakness—but I love his memory. I do not mourn without hope—he is happy now, and his aches and pains are over.

Reuben. Yes, he is happy now. But do you know, Eliza, when his little heart was changed? I think it was during our Sabbath-school revival last year.

Eliza. On the 16th day of January, I believe. During his sickness he was very patient, and I am told was never heard to murmur, but often heard to pray. His great desire was to go to heaven; and when inquired of who he loved best, he would always reply, Jesus. At times when his sufferings were extreme, he would exclaim, "O blessed Jesus, take me to thyself above where pleasure never dies." When asked whether he did not wish to get well and stay with mother, he replied, "Rather die and go to heaven." And did you hear, Reuben, what he told his mother? "Mother," said he, "God is not a spirit to those that are heaven, only to those that are on earth." His mother then asked him if he had anything to say to the teachers. "Tell them to tell the children to get ready and meet me in heaven." "I wish every person knew," he would say, "what a beautiful place heaven is—what a glorious place—the houses are made of silver, and the streets are paved with gold." After a short sleep one day, he awoke in great pain.— "At twelve o'clock, my dear," said his mother, "I believe you will leave us, and this afternoon your spirit will be in heaven." "Oh," said he, "I wish this morning,—I will soon go home! I will soon go home."

Alfred. I have heard, Eliza, he was very prompt and correct in answering the questions that were put to him. For instance,—What did Christ say concerning little children? "Suffer little children to come unto me," &c. What did Christ do to little children? "He took them up in his arms and blessed them." What has the Lord promised in that day when he will make up his jewels?— "To those on the right hand, he will say, Come, ye blessed of my Father, inherit the kingdom prepared for you from the foundation of the world—and to those on the left, Depart from me, ye cursed, into everlasting fire."

Reuben. Yes, and don't you recollect the answer he made to the question: What must we do to inherit eternal life: "Love God," said he, "with all thy heart, with all thy mind, with all thy strength, and thy neighbor as thyself." And one night when his mother's heart found comfort in tears, after she had sung to the little suffering boy "Jesus can make a dying bed feel soft as downy pillows are"—" Why do you cry, mother?" said he—" Don't be afraid—I wish we could both go to heaven to-night—I shall go." But, John, what will you do there? "Sing the song of Moses and the Lamb," said he,—and when the cold hands of the Destroyer were feeling for his life-pulse, and his little heart was quivering in the strong folds of death—" Have you any view of heaven, John?" inquired his mother—" Yes, ma'am," said he, "and a very bright one too." In a few hours he expired, " gentle and undefiled," leaving with us a bright testimony that he has gone to dwell with Jesus.

Alfred. Were you at his funeral, Eliza? It appears to me I did not see you there. And do you remember his looks as he lay in his little coffin—how sweet a smile played on his face—how natural his hair was parted *here*—how his little hands were clasped on his bosom—and how like an angel he appeared?

Eliza. Yes, I had the satisfaction, Alfred, of seeing him before he was buried. Carried by the hands of his school-mates we followed him to the church-yard, *there* to await the period when the " mortal shall put on immortality"—when soul and body, " in a moment, in the twinkling of an eye, at the last trump" shall be reunited. He has gone, brother Alfred, to "the better world"—he is no longer in his earthly father's house—at the family altar—he no longer will be seen in our Sabbath-school—and "the place that knew him once will know him no more forever."

> "Approving smiles caressed thee,
>   Where'er thy footsteps roved;
> The ear that heard thee blessed thee,
>   The eye that saw thee loved.
> And though the shadowy valley,
>   With Death's dark frown was dim,
> Light cheered the stormy passage,
>   And thou art safe with Him."

Reuben. I think, Eliza, I have something you would be delighted to see. I have kept it now almost a year. It does me good to look at it, and I hope always to keep it as a memento of one who will long have a place in my affections. It is a ringlet of his hair. Here it is.

Alfred. I almost envy you, Reuben, in this respect; though I suppose it is useless to ask for a lock.

Girl (in the gallery). So do I—I would give most anything for it. I went to school with little Johnny.

Eliza. I am not envious, for I expect to meet him in heaven. I expect to enjoy his company there, and share at the same banquet. I expect to strike hands on the banks of deliverance. I expect to meet many there whom I knew in the flesh. I expect to meet our teacher and two scholars there. Reuben will you meet me there? Alfred, will you meet me there? Teachers, Superintendents and Ministers, will you meet me there? Children, will you meet me there? Fathers, mothers, sisters, brothers, let us meet each other there.

TO ———.

WRITTEN IN THE BLANK LEAF OF A BIBLE.

Be this thy Guide! In all thy ways
   Be this thy Chart forever—
'Twill lead thee through life's sinful maze,
On the dear Saviour's face to gaze
   When friends no more shall sever.

Take with thee, ———, take this light
   By our kind Father given—
'Twill prove a Beacon, day and night,
Whose cheerful rays keep ever bright
   The Christian's path to heaven.

NEW-YEAR HYMN.

With the opening year
In His courts we appear,
Who hath brought us safe through
His kind acts to review,—
Now to join in the praise
Of the "Ancient of Days,"
Let our voices ascend
With the heart's joyful lays.
Happy New-Year, dear friends! we meet you again,
To return our thanksgivings, Amen and amen!
Then with heart and with voice, ye children, rejoice!
Happy New-Year! happy New-Year! Amen and amen!

We have come to repeat
Our glad songs at Thy feet,
And confess Thy kind hand
Hath been o'er our young band—
While temptations abound
In our paths all around,
A refuge from evil
In Sabbath-school's found.
Chorus—Happy New-Year, dear friends, &c.

We are now on our way,
And can make no delay,
To yon blissful abode
With the saints of the Lord;
There our teachers we'll meet,
And with them have a seat,
When our New-Years all end
In that blissful retreat.
Chorus—Happy New-Year, dear friends! &c.

SURPRISE ADDRESS.

ASKING FOR A SPEECH.

[Seven little boys and girls successively follow each other, and standing before the Pastor while seated, repeat]

1. We are coming now, dear Pastor!
    About one hundred strong—
 We are coming from the Sabbath-school
    To help your cause along.
2. We are coming now, dear Pastor!
    When you have passed away,
 We will take our Teachers' places,
    And work as hard as they.
3. We are coming now, dear Pastor!
    Upon life's busy stage;
 We'll look to God and do our part
    To bless the coming age.
4. We are coming now, dear Pastor!
    To labor for the Lord,
 When you have gone to heaven
    To gain the great reward.
5. We are coming now, dear Pastor!
    There's work for us to do—
 The harvest fields are ripening fast,
    And laborers are few.
6. We are coming now, dear Pastor!
    To give you Christmas cheer:
 To bless you, and caress you
    With a kiss of love sincere.
7. We are coming now, dear Pastor!
    Not to hear you preach;
 But my Teachers wish you'd condescend
    To make a little speech.

RECITATION.

BY A BOY.

TO A MOTHER MOURNING THE LOSS OF HER CHILDREN.

MOTHER! where are thy children? where
    Those tender plants—the three
Who used in other days to share
    Your watchful sympathy?
Not long ago, around the hearth
    Their cheerful smiles were seen—
Where are they now? Beneath the earth,
    Where droops the willow green?

Ah, no! you should not call them dead!
    The caskets may decay:
Their spirits to a house have fled
    That ne'er shall pass away.
"Suffer these little ones to come
    To Me"—the Saviour spake—
And now in heaven they have a home
    They never will forsake.

Two gentle girls, and noble boy,
    You reared awhile with care—
They filled thy humble cot with joy,
    And made it happy there.
Their little hymns—their fond " good-night,"
    All linger with thee yet:

And Memory keeps within thy sight
    What other hearts forget.

Father! where are thy loved ones now,
    The idols of thy heart?
Saw'st thou Death's image on their brow?
    And did the tear-drops start?
Forget it not—'Twas God's own call
    To place that heart above—
His terms of life are—*all for all*—
    Oh! give Him all thy love.

Brother! have thy companions gone?
    Their fragile forms no more
Will join with thee, at night and morn,
    Around the open door.
The years pass on—and thou art here—
    One only sister left!
But angel watchers hover near
    The kindred now bereft.

Commend yourselves to God—and say,
    "Thy will on earth be done,
Who gave, and early took away,
    Our jewels, one by one."
Not willingly He sends His rod—
    He chastens whom He saves—
Oh! yield your hearts in faith to God
    Beside your children's graves.

MY FIRST "EXTEMPORE."

BY AN INFANT CLASS SCHOLAR.

LITTLE BOYS AND GIRLS AS BIG AS ME :—I likes to see you. It makes me feel real glad. I had a real nice dinner to-day; and I had some candies in my stockings last night too, and some little funny things. Oh! how you would laugh! Pa says perhaps Santa Claus, that loves little boys, came down the hole where the smoke goes up. But I think that was funny, 'cause my candies was clean white! I love that man, don't you? But I don't love him best of every body. I love my pa and ma, and all my friends and relations. And every night I say my prayers. I love to say my prayers, don't you? My ma undresses me every night, and then I kneel down in her lap real nice. I love my ma, don't you? And then I say,—" Now I lay me down to sleep," and some more. Ma says God, the Father, loves little boys and girls. And I love God, don't you? Mamma says God the Father takes care of little boys like me, and gives us new jackets and trowsers and every thing. My pa says Jesus was born to-day, a good while ago. And he says that Jesus died for me and every body. Ain't that too bad?— Poor Jesus! He says he died 'cause he wanted me to be good, and love every body and go to heaven—way up in the sky—where the "beautiful sunset" is. And by and by, my ma says, if I be good and don't tell stories, and stay away from the fire, and love Jesus and every body, Jesus will send an angel and take me away up in the sky, further than a balloon. And I'm going to be good. Ain't you? You must say "Yes." Well, you *can* go if you be good, and love Jesus and God the Father, and every body.

Ain't this nice to be here? and see all these people dressed up? and all this light? First Christmas ever I remember. I'm real glad to see you, little children like me. I didn't know little children dressed in white here. I thought all little children dressed in white were in heaven. This ain't heaven, is it? You ain't angels, are you? Oh! no, I 'member now—ma says angels have crowns and palms in their hands. You havn't got 'em, has you! No, all you'se got to die and be put in coffins. Won't your mothers feel real bad? In heaven it will be a good deal better than it is here. There will be more people—and it will be ever so much lighter; and my ma says she has one—three—four little children up in heaven; and one of these days, she says, I may go see them—but she says she don't want me to go now. I guess there's a good many mothers here got little children up there. Ma says every body will fly like birds, and have dresses whiter than my night-gown. I want to go to heaven and be an angel—and see Jesus and God the Father, and every body.—Don't you? Well, you may. But you musn't make any body cry. My pa wants me now. Good bye!

RECITATION.

BY A GIRL.

OUR PASTOR'S WIFE.

Alas! my soul! aga'n 'tis said
A wife—a mother—friend—is dead—
A spirit, pure as earth possess'd,
From mortal ills has gone to rest;
By faith she lived the present life—
In hope has died our pastor's wife.

But late, she trod the Church's aisle,
With graceful step and placid smile;
And now a vacant seat I view,
Where she has knelt in worship true
Before the Lord—her God in life—
The Saviour of our pastor's wife.

But late, we met for social prayer,
And she we mourn was also there;
In grateful words she told her love—
Her expectations, soon above

To join the ransomed host in life—
The theme that charmed our pastor's wife.

Though fell consumption, many years,
Prey'd on her in this "vale of tears"—
Though pale the cheek, and weak the frame,
The soul was calm—the heart a flame—
One purpose ruled 'mid nature's strife,
One object sought our pastor's wife.

And now, a circle of kind friends
Their grief with orphan children blends;
In sorrow o'er a grave they weep
Where a fond mother's ashes sleep:
Oh! be it theirs to walk through life
As spotless as our pastor's wife.

Another heart is pierced and sore—
Another mourner's standing o'er
Her sleeping bed, with tearful eye—
He fain would choose like her to lie,
With whom he's spent the best of life—
His consort, and our pastor's wife.

Yet say, belov'd—"Thy will be done!"
Thy Christian race will soon be run—
In union blest, more full and sweet,
Thy dear companion thou wilt meet,
Where death is swallow'd up of life—
Thy blissful home—our pastor's wife.

GREETING TO THE PASTOR.

BY AN INFANT SCHOLAR.

Mr. Preacher! how do you do?
I have come to speak to you—
Glad to see you on our stage,
Youth and venerable age.

'Tis my mission to express
These little children's thankfulness
For your toil and constant care
In our School, and every where.

Each Sabbath-day we see you come
To our pleasant Sabbath home;
And the boys and girls rejoice
When they hear their Pastor's voice.

Grateful feelings prompt me now
To come forward with my bow:
And say to all who here attend,
The Pastor is the children's friend!

Plain and truthful is your teaching,
Urgent—simple—kind your preaching:
May the seed you scatter here
In our future lives appear.

RECITATION.

ON THE DEATH OF AN AGED MINISTER.

BY A BOY OR GIRL.

"I cleave to my Saviour!" the patriarch saith,
As he stood on the borders—the Jordan of Death—
Though cold were its waters, and darksome the grave,
No fears filled his bosom, for Jesus would save.

His three score of years, and his locks white as snow,
Gave token his days were near spent below—
His mission was ended—life's pilgrimage o'er—
The Master has called him, to suffer no more.

"I cleave to my Saviour!" our teacher and friend
So whispered in faith as he drew near his end:
In a land far remote amid strangers he sleeps,
While the Church he so cherish'd in sorrow now weeps.

For whom was he toiling?—His soul could not rest
Till with a free Gospel the heathen were blest—
Those "sitting in darkness" became his chief care,
For such were his labors, his journeys, and prayer.

"I cleave to my Saviour!"—In Him was his trust
To meet in God's kingdom and reign with the just:
He has lived for His glory—the Truth to proclaim—
He has died giving honor to Jesus' sweet name.

We hasten on, father!—Thy voice we yet hear
In promptings to duty as death is so near—
And soon with our pastor, redeemed we shall come
To mingle our praises, in Canaan---at home.

DIALOGUE.

"IN WANT OF A SUBJECT."

BY A BOY AND GIRL.

Stephen. I declare, Frances, it is as much as my head is worth to get through this crowd.

Frances. Well, Stephen, perhaps it is. I have no right to doubt your word; but why did you venture your head, Stephen? I didn't send for you.

S. Why, Frances, I thought you would expect me, as we have been in the habit of talking together at our anniversary for many years. But if you don't want me, I can go. [Turning his back.]

F. There, now, don't get affronted, Master Stephen. I didn't mean to hurt your feelings. I should like very well to talk with you if you have anything new to communicate.

S. Nothing very new, Frances. "There's nothing new under the sun." In fact, I don't know what to talk about. I never was at such a loss for a subject "in all my born days;" but I expect as we proceed, one thought will bring on another, and if we can't do any better, we'll make a "chowder" on 't before we get through. I never study my sermons like some folks.

F. If you don't "study your sermons," Stephen, you ought to have a text on such an occasion as this. I believe this congregation is too intelligent to like your "chowder," Stephen, and I therefore propose to take a definite subject to discuss. What say you, Stephen?

S. I don't know about that, Frances. I guess I ain't got learning enough to hold a discussion, especially if it requires much thinking, for I tell you the crowd has nearly crowded my wits out, Frances, and I ain't accustomed to debate either.

F. Well, Stephen, I think the subject I have to propose will suit you. It's a very important one to be settled to-night. It has a direct bearing on the interests of our school, and should be attended to by somebody. And what do you think it is, Stephen?

S. I suppose from its having "a *direct* bearing on the interests of our school," you mean money. But you may depend upon it, Frances, the people won't thank you for it.

F. No matter for that, Stephen, we'll thank them.

I have often heard brother J—— say he "hated to talk about money," and for fear he should neglect it, let us choose this subject for our conversation together. And first, Stephen, let me ask you how much people pay when they go to the theatre?

S. I never was there myself. The big bills in the streets say, "Pit, 50 cents—Boxes, $1." But I don't believe there is anybody here who visits such places, and your question, therefore, is hardly suitable, Frances.

F. I didn't say there was; but if worldly people give fifty cents to go into a pit, Christians ought to give fifty cents to keep out of it; and if worldly people give fifty cents for so much chaff, Christians ought to give a dollar for as much wheat; and if worldly people give fifty cents, and a dollar even, to see men and women mimic the sayings and doings of others, Christians ought to give more to see the original actors themselves, especially when acting on the stage of moral and religious improvement.

S. Sure enough, Frances, but don't you know worldly-minded people give more to support the "lusts of the eye and the pride of life," than professed Christians do to spread the Gospel, or advance the happiness of the immortal soul, and the glory of the Redeemer?

F. 'Tis so, I know very well. And now the second question I want to ask you is this: how much money ought we to have to carry on our Sabbath-school enterprise next year? Have you ever "counted the cost," Stephen?

S. No, I never did. But it takes a good deal, I guess.

F. Well, I have. It's something like house-keeping, only we have more in family than most folks, and nobody knows the wants of a family till they get one. The difference is, the Sabbath-school furnishes food for the mind, or soul, and the plates we use are books, which, though they don't get broken, with much using they often wear out, and then we must have new ones. And as our school increases in number, which is the fact, we want a larger quantity.

S. But ain't there other things needed, Frances, beside books?

F. Certainly there are. Some children in this Sabbath-school family need shoes and clothing and hats and bonnets. Good children are rewarded to encourage them and keep them good. We need fuel in winter, and there are various things, "too numerous to mention."

S. How much then, Frances, ought you to have

next year? As you have "counted the cost," you can tell me, no doubt.

F. Not less than $100. The theatres will take in their thousands to-night, and it's a pity, I think, if the Sabbath-school can't have the small sum of $100; and if our preacher was any kind of a beggar, we'd get it, too.

S. "Beggar," Frances! You don't call it begging, to ask the church to support the Sabbath-school, do you? I don't.

F. No, Stephen, that's a wrong word. I didn't mean to use it—but I want him to make a speech, and a real strong one, and "make no bones about it." The money we want, and the money we ought to have. It will encourage the teachers, and you'll see, next year, how much good it will do.

S. By the way, Frances, I'll ask the third question. Why don't the Sabbath-school get as much money in this church as they do in others? Can you tell me?

F. Some folks sell tickets of admission, but our teachers think it looks too much like going to a "poppet show," and don't do it. In some churches, the ladies and gentlemen set together in the same seat, and when they go to a Sabbath-school exhibition, if the wife has forgotten to bring her purse, she can ask her husband for some change, and he can't refuse in a public congregation. It wouldn't look husband-like, you know!

S. No, not at all, Frances. And then you think if the ladies and gentlemen in this church were to sit together, we would get more money, do you?

F. No doubt of it, Stephen. And how much more sociable and pleasing it would look! As it is, one goes out of one door, and the other the other, and the lady may find her husband if she can, or the husband his lady. In the evening, the engine-boy may insult her or puff smoke in her face if she is alone. There would be less running down stairs during preaching, less tobacco chewing, less whispering among the young men, and more money, Stephen, and I'm in favor of *change*.

S. But to make the change you speak of, Frances, would be removing old landmarks, and we should *unmethodize* the church.

F. Not at all, Stephen, we don't intend to be first. We shall only follow in the "footsteps of our illustrious predecessors." We don't intend to sell the pews, but have a free Methodist church—and I tell you I'm in favor of a reform. The majority can do it, and we'll put it to vote. Now, children, you that are in favor of your parents sitting together in church, raise your hands. [All raise hands.] Contrary sign—carried. Good night, Stephen.

S. You have made a better "chowder" than I could, Frances. Good night.

RECITATION.

BY A BOY.

YOUNG DAVID'S SLING AND STONE.

My Teacher said I might come here,
    "If I knew *what* to speak"—
But "there's the rub"—I'm not so clear—
I've nothing new to please the ear,
    Beside, my voice is weak.

Though but a boy, I hear and see
    How sin is growing strong—
For instance, you will all agree
That in this "land of LIBERTY"
    All Slavery is wrong.

I look with tearful eyes around,
    And evils meet my sight—
The wicked prosper and abound,
Intemp'rance every where is found,
    And Satan rules the night.

'Tis sad to see how vile and base
    The human may become!
I wonder God should save a race
Whose ways bring sorrow and disgrace,
    Through Passion—Lust—and Rum!

Up, friends! awake! let God be heard!
    Your Maker's voice obey—
Oh! hear Him speaking in His word—
Let Christian hearts with love be stirred,
    And labor while you may.

You may prevail! Resolve to try!
    In Jesus' name begin,—
Let not "the harvest time" go by,
The "summer end," when you must die,
    And leave this world in sin.

Let me—a child—to-night appeal
    For those by Satan bound—
Think what the Judgment will reveal!
Oh, man of God! for sinners feel
    Before the trump shall sound.

Let me—a child—take David's stand
    The giant to destroy,—
The sins that triumph in our land,
In every form, on every hand—
    I would, though but a boy,
With "sling and stone" in Heaven's might
Reform the Wrong, and aid the Right.

INFANT-CLASS HYMN.

Tune—"WE ARE ON OUR WAY."

Here we come, an infant band,
        Marching on—
Soldiers to the promised land,
        Marching on—
Thus we spend the day—sweetly singing,
        One and all—
Here we learn to pray—humbly kneeling,
        One and all.

To Sabbath-school we're going,
        Moving on—
Where knowledge free is flowing,
        To the young:
Teachers! lead the way—souls are dying,
        All around!
Let us not delay—time is flying—
        Till the ground!

Come, children! join the chorus,
        Swell the song!
The crown is just before us—
        Move along!
Soon we will arise—glory! glory!
        Safe above—
And in yonder skies, tell the story
        Of His love!

Here wisdom we're receiving
>From the Lord;
And taught to be believing
In His Word.
Schoolmates! will you come, knowledge seeking,
Grace and truth?
"Find in Me a home!" Christ is speaking,
In your youth!

DIALOGUE.

THE FATHERLESS AND MOTHERLESS.

BY FOUR GIRLS.

[*Mary* is reading her Bible, and *Cecelia* is looking for her Sunday Proofs, at a table. Singing by two voices, plaintively, in the gallery—"*I never clasp a friendly hand,*" &c.]

Cecelia. Hark, Mary! that singing reminds me of the serenades last night. Did you hear them about midnight, how sweetly their voices sounded in the quiet streets, when most everybody had gone to bed?

Mary. I heard them, sister, and was delighted—it called to my mind the New Year's eves when father and mother were living. Don't you remember, Cecelia, how sweetly we were serenaded last year? They then sang father's favorite tune— and though he was so poorly, he seemed so pleased

Cecelia. I was so little then, Mary, I don't recollect what tune you mean. I should like to learn the tune father loved—I think I should sing it often. What was its name, Mary? Won't you sing it for me?

Mary. It affects me so much when I hear it, since your father and mother died. You must feel very lonesome, do you not?

Phoebe, aside. Why, Frances, how you talk! You do not mean to say that Mrs. L—— is dead too, do you? and that Cecelia, and Mary, and the other children are now entire orphans? I knew that Mr. L—— died last February, but I want to know if their poor mother has followed the father so soon!

Frances. Oh, yes, Phoebe, she died in August following, and they are now sleeping in the same grave-yard, side by side. She was quite delicate and feeble at the time of Mr. L——'s death, and immediately after went into a decline, which has terminated in the orphanage of her little household. I remember the day well, when she leaned over the cold remains of her husband, in the church, and with an almost breaking heart, fell back in her chair, as they bore his coffin from her view. *That* was a time for tears, Phoebe—they had been united so many years—had shared together in so many blessings and Providences—and had been surrounded with such a large family, which were then to be left without the advice and admonitions of a pious, praying father—that I do not wonder she felt the stroke severely. Beside, he had been an invalid for eighteen months, and had required and received her attentions, like a helpless child, so long, it is not strange if her love for her poor husband had grown even stronger than otherwise, and the parting time more keenly felt. She then said, " She could not live, and be parted from her Charles "— and true enough, she very soon followed him to " yonder world of spirits bright," to taste its pleasures and its joys to share.

    There, Mary, your dear parents live,
        Released from every pain—
    Like them, your heart to Jesus give,
        And you shall meet again.
    There, Cele, pa has gone to dwell,
        With sister, and with brother,
    You'll never hear the word " farewell,"
        When you yet home with mother.

Phœbe. No, no, dear girls, this dress of mourning for those who loved you best, will then be changed for a robe of white, with which the "spirits of the just" are clothed. Our habitations will not be left desolate any more, nor will the funeral knell bring sorrow to the lone and widowed heart. The thousands of children, like yourselves, who have been parted on earth from the embrace of parental love and affection, may again be united in the heavenly world—and oh! how happy will be that meeting, when it will be said by your father and mother—"Here, Lord, are we, and the children thou gavest us." Here is your consolation, girls, and here is your hope, as an anchor to the soul—"Jesus hath died that we might live," and hath gone to prepare mansions for us, that where he is, there we may be also.

> Then dry your tears—no longer weep—
> Your friends in Jesus sweetly sleep:
> Say not they're dead—you yet will find
> Death cannot quench the soul—the mind.
> 'Twill wake, when Gabriel's trump shall blow,
> And all that sleep to judgment go.
> Then brother Charles will leave his bed,
> And rise with Christ, his "living head."
> From North and South, from East and West,
> The good will rise—forever blest.

Oh! I love, Frances, to think of the resurrection—what a solemn, yet glorious day methinks it will be.

Frances. Yes, Phoebe, but not a "glorious day" to those who live in sin, and leave the world unprepared. It will be glorious to those who have walked in obedience with God on earth—who have kept the faith—and have died in peace. And such, I can safely say, was the character of brother Charles L———. He was a man of prayer—with his heart he worshiped the God whom he served—with his lips he commended to others the religion he professed, and by his daily walk gave evidence of his sincerity. I am not apt to eulogize the dead, but here—*here* are his witnesses. This sanctuary has echoed the thousand hosannas of his soul. Here he labored—here he prayed—and his constant attendance said to all, "Come, let us go up to the house of the Lord."

Emma. I knew Mr. L———, Frances. He used always to be at church on Sunday, whether it rained or shined—and used to come into our Sunday-school, too, more times than our minister and other members does. I used to love him.

Phoebe. I have heard, Frances, that he experienced religion when he was quite young. Do you know how old he was at the time? Perhaps the statement may encourage others to "go and do likewise."

Frances. He was between sixteen and seventeen years of age, if I am correctly informed—while yet in "the heat of youthful blood,"—when he gave his heart to the Saviour, and found religion so good, that the allurements of the world could never induce him to forsake the Lord, or "cast his word behind." He was a useful working member of the church—and if any are now present who composed the original band, they can tell you how he stood, as was said in his funeral sermon, "like the beaten anvil to the stroke." Ah! how limited the number now left. Let them be called, and oh! how few will answer. Dear friends! your companions have left you—they have passed from earth to heaven. They who once cheered and encouraged you to faithfulness in those meetings and the sanctuary here, are beckoning you still to persevere. Hark! did you hear the last words of brother Charles?— While he was racked with pains, and the last breath was hurrying to be away from his emaciated frame, he cried, "Glory! glory! glory!" Yes, friends! he had glory in view while living, and had it, no doubt, revealed to him when dying, and from glory he is to-night looking down upon those he loved in the flesh.

Phoebe, looking up. And well did he love our little Sabbath-school. I remember when he came here at our last Anniversary, and sat in *that* pew—weak and tremulous, and wrapped in his cloak. He said "the very sight of the dear children made him feel better"—he loved to see them, and hear their tender voices lisping his Saviour's praises—and is not his spirit to-night hovering over us, and his orphan children?

>Say, do not seraph spirits come,
>And hover o'er their once loved home?
>If so, I'm sure L———'s here,
>And will be, every opening year.

Frances. We have said nothing, thus far, Phoebe, to his associates in the church. And to whom first shall I speak? Many I see around me who have taken sweet council with the departed L———. Here are his class companions, who used to listen to the warm breathings of his soul, as he told them week after week of his Lord's dealings—of the trials he had met and overcome by the way—of the strong faith he had in his blessed Saviour—and how he expected to be caught up by and by to see "the King in his glory." Did you not hear him sing "We'll march around Jerusalem"? and did you not join together in the chorus, "Oh that will be joyful"? Yes, often have ye prayed together, and sung together, and your hearts rejoiced together in thankfulness and hope ; and those seasons have all passed away—that voice is silent and those lips are sealed to us. The memory of other days, when you met too in the tented grove, will often move the heart and awaken devotion. You there saw him laboring for his and others' good, and spending his little strength for souls. Did you mark the paleness of his brow, the subdued tone, and the feeble step, when you met him last at the encampment? He will meet you there no more.— The summer may come, and the shrub and tree again put forth, and you may assemble yourselves in the peaceful wood for prayer—you may come to your class, and sit in the seat where he was wont, but Charles will not be there. Ah, no! he has gone from the "church militant to the church triumphant"—from this vale of tears, as he said, "to his other home." Follow him, as he followed Christ, and you will meet him there. And here, too, are the Trustees of the church. You have the name of Charles L—— on your records. He was once of your number. Have you not missed him in your monthly meetings? When clouds and darkness seemed to gather over you, and fears for the prosperity of your little Zion took hold on some, have ye not heard him say, "Brethren, don't give up the ship—the Lord will send us deliverance?" Was he not always at his post while he could, to devise, and encourage, and counsel with you? Yes, brethren! but now you see his face no more. He rests from his labors.

>   Life's toilsome way he's traveled o'er,
>   And bore the heavy load—
>   But Christ hath led his weary feet
>   To reach his blest abode.
>   And when the Lord shall summon us,
>   Whom thou hast left behind—
>   May we, untainted by the world,
>   As sure a welcome find.

To the members of the church in general, I would say, you have met with him for the last time around this altar. Look, bereaved friends! do you not see him in your minds slowly bending his steps to the Lord's table? Do you not hear his grateful soul breaking out in "hallelujahs," as, for the last last time, he kneels? He is now drinking the wine of the kingdom anew in glory.

>   We'll leave him there—the guest of love,
>   Released, redeemed and free:
>   We'll strive to meet the good above,
>   And then we'll meet with thee.

SONG OF THE POOR.

Written for an Industrial School.

Tune—"LILLY DALE."

"Despise not the poor because he is poor,"
    Says a Voice from the LAWGIVER'S Book—
That Voice is heard, and men's heart's are stirr'd,
    As Pity's meek eyes on us look.
        Dear Teachers! kind Teachers!
        Friends of the Poor!
Our love we'll express, and thy names we will bless,
    While the mem'ry of youth shall endure.

We have no happy home from whence we have come,
    Where Comfort and Plenty abound—
But wants daily rise without its supplies,
    And Sorrow is brooding around.
        Dear Teachers! kind Teachers! &c.

Oh! thankful are we our patrons to see,
    The almoners to Poverty's caste,—
The work is begun, and the lone orphan'd one
    Finds refuge and succor at last.
        Dear Teachers! kind Teachers! &c.

Kind Charity's hand an asylum has plann'd,
  Where the Children of Penury meet—
And lessons of Truth we are learning in youth,
  In this favor'd and friendly retreat.
    Dear Teachers! kind Teachers! &c.

When years roll around, and your brows shall be crown'd
  With the silvery emblems of age,
This now feeble band in your places may stand,
  And the sorrows of others assuage.
    Dear Teachers! kind Teachers, &c.

THE CHILDREN'S WISHES.

[The speakers present themselves separately before the pastor, and then stand in a row until he rises to speak.]

GIRL.   We greet you, Pastor! and rejoice
        That *we* have both a tongue and voice—
        Through them we hope to fill your ear
        With our good wishes this New-Year.

BOY.   I wish the Lord may give you grace
        To preach the Gospel in this place—
        To give the trump that certain call
        That shall engage the hearts of all.

THE CHILDREN'S WISHES.

GIRL. I wish He would the power bestow
Error and sin to overthrow—
Till every Church shall "rise and shine,"
And prove its authorship Divine.

BOY. I wish the cause for which you pray
May make new conquests every day;
That by each sermon preached this year
Glad souls may start for heaven here.

GIRL. I wish our Sabbath-School could feel
More Christian love and burning zeal
To save the children—bring them in
From the dark paths of vice and sin.

BOY. I wish our Country was at peace,
That War and Discord soon may cease:
That Union arms may win the fight,
And Uncle Sam come out "all right."
I wish the President but knew
Our teachers here both tried and true,
I know he 'd give them a command
To drive the rebels from the land.

GIRL. I wish before we close this meeting,
And leave this joyous, happy greeting,
To ask a favor—and beseech
Our Minister to make a SPEECH.

"LITTLE TWIGS."

Tune—"PRETTY LITTLE ZEPHYRS WE."

Tender "Little Twigs" are we
  In the vineyard of the Lord;
Fruitful vines we'd like to be,
  On the arbor of His word.

May each "Little Twig" be bent
  In the way that it should be,
So it shall be evident
  It will make an upright tree.

By and by the frost will come—
  But the Vine will never die:
Then transplanted we'll go home
  To the gardens of the sky.

There will be an endless spring,
  Dews of love will ever fall;
Children choirs will sweetly sing
  Praises to the Lord of All.

"Little Twigs" we'll be no more;
  Blossoms now, then fruit will be:
Angels 'round the throne we'll soar—
  God's bright throne of Purity.

Tender "Little Twigs" are we
  Clinging to the parent Vine,
Sweetly making melody
  To the Son of God divine.   JR.

CHRISTMAS ADDRESS.

BY A BOY.

Christians and Friends of the Sabbath-school:

My duty, in the order of our juvenile exercises to-night, is to deliver the opening address. It requires considerable nerve to be " the first speaker." To stand up before such an audience, older in years, in experience and judgment, seems like vanity on my part, and makes me blush and tremble with fear. The position I occupy is not of my own seeking, friends! I am placed here by our Teachers, to express their sentiments and feelings, in their behalf to bid you welcome to our Christmas festivities—to meet you one and all on the very threshold of our Annual Jubilee with thanks for your interest in the Sabbath-school cause, which your presence indicates, and to wish you a joyous Christmas night in compensation for your " material aid " to our empty treasury.

I premise that the influence for good and benofits of the Sabbath-school institution are points conceded by every person present. With such a system of supervision over the moral, intellectual and social character as the Sunday-school provides—with the free use of a library judiciously selected and circulated through the neighborhood—in the study of a text-book gratuitously furnished, of such universal interest and value as the BIBLE—under the tuition of those whose services are entirely voluntary and uncompensated, and rendered from the most benevolent and honorable motives, on a day when neither teachers nor pupils could be prosecuting worldly business without a violation of human and divine law,—and all designed and calculated to qualify them to serve their generation in the fear of God in all the relations of life, and to prepare them for perfect and endless glory, " when all these things shall be dissolved,"—we venture to declare the Sunday-school the cheapest, the most efficient, and most rational system of education which the ingenuity of man has ever devised.

God has honored its instrumentality in thousands of conversions. Its restraining power is felt and seen in every city, town, and village, in keeping children from Sabbath violations and evil company, and the catechism and Scripture proofs and pious biography and other good books are occupying and engrossing minds which would otherwise be seeking other paths for amusement and recreation. Its effects have been blessed wherever established. The church is deriving her "men of strength" from these nurseries of Christianity, and the falling ranks of her veterans in the crusade against sin are constantly being filled from this noble "reserve corps." The missionary fields white for the harvest are obtaining laborers from among former Sabbath-school scholars, men who are "taking their lives in their hands" for the object of saving souls and glorifying God. Such is the institution and cause I represent to-night. Let me commend it to your continued sympathy and prayers. Let the church, if she would increase in piety and zeal, and rise in the sublimity of her power, foster this branch of religious education. Let the ministry give its encouragement, the laity its helping hand, and the fathers and mothers follow up at home the holy influence of the Sabbath-school, and the result will be mighty in pulling down the strong holds of the evil one. Thank God for the Sabbath-school! Thanks to the men and women who give it their time and support. Its destiny, its usefulness, its achievements, its triumphs are not yet effected. After your aching heads and time-worn frames, dear teachers, are lying in the grave-yard, the work will go on. When you, our dear pastor, shall be praising God in heaven, amid anthems of redeeming love, the Sabbath-school will be preparing others to fill vacant pulpits. When you, our beloved teachers, have finished the work God has given you to do, and you pass to your reward, from this little band of loving hearts will rise up many "to call you blessed."

> 'Tis not in vain you give your strength,
>   Your time, your patience here—
> The ripen'd fruit we'll see at length,
>   The harvest home is near.
> A little while the toil endure,
>   The heat and burden bear—
> The faithful shall the crown secure,
>   The palm of victory wear.

My time is limited, and I must leave these thoughts with you. Let me now speak of the day we celebrate. We are always ready for "Merry Christmas." It comes laden with precious memories to the aged, and with cheerfulness to the young. Let us remember it not only as a day of feasting and merriment, but as a holy day. Upon this day, in a country far from this and many hundred years ago, God sent down from heaven the most precious gift the world ever did or ever will receive. It was a lovely night; and out in the fields a company of shepherds were watching their flocks. All day they had wandered with them, but at evening they were gathered in a fold, while the shepherds in their midst were resting on the ground. Suddenly a bright light appeared in the sky, so strange and so bright they were afraid. A beautiful angel with shining wings came flying down, and told them that he had come to bring them a message of great joy. He said there was that day born in Bethlehem a Saviour, and that they would find the babe lying in a manger. The air was filled with angels, singing, " Glory to God, and on earth peace, good will to men." The shepherds walked into Bethlehem to find out the meaning of this. There lay the babe in sweet unconsciousness upon a bed of straw in the manger where cattle were fed, for there was no room at the inn for his poor and humble parents.— That little bed of straw was a more glorious place than a kingly cradle. The very sky looked on rejoicingly, for a new star appeared over the spot where the infant was laid. A very wicked man named Herod was king at that time. When he heard of all this he was angry, for he thought this child might grow up to be the king in his palace.

He called some of his wise men to him, and sent them to look for the babe, and then come and tell him where he was. So the wise men took some presents and started in their search, and the new star moved along before them until it stood still over the place where they found the child. They knelt down before him, and gave Mary his mother the presents which they had brought. God was watching over this precious little one, and would not call on the wicked Herod to find him, but directed the wise men in their dreams at night not to go back to Herod, but to return to their homes another way. The day upon which he was born is called Christmas, from his name Christ and Mass, which means a feast or holy day. One Christmas night, two hundred and eighty-four years after the shepherds found the babe in Bethlehem, a company of those who loved to remember Christ were singing hymns and praising God for this great gift to man. They were called Christians as a name of reproach, for in number they were poor and despised. While they were assembled, the Roman Emperor, named Dioclesian, sent a company of soldiers to surround the church, and then set fire to the building, and they were all burned to ashes and buried beneath the fallen walls! How different is our situation to-night! How favored are we, who can worship the same Jesus where none can "molest or make us afraid!" We celebrate to-night the birth of the world's Redeemer, he who cured the leper, the sick, the palsied—who touched the bier of the widow's son and said— "Young man, arise," and he rose up and spoke— who quieted the tempest, and healed the daughter of Jarius, and opened the eyes of the blind, and fed five thousand by a miracle—who walked on the sea, and raised Lazarus from the dead—who took little children in his arms and blessed them—who smote the barren fig-tree and cast the money-changers out of the temple, and foretold the destruction of Jerusalem—who in an agony prayed in the Garden of Gethsemane until great drops of sweat fell down from his face to the ground—who was betrayed and made prisoner and crucified—who was buried, and on the third day arose from the grave and ascended to heaven, there to make intercession for us.

Be it ours to love the Saviour; and when we cease his praises here, may you and I, and these my dear companions in the Sabbath-school, go where he has gone to reign in eternal glory, from whence he watches those who love him upon earth, and hears their prayers and soothes their sorrows. In His kind keeping I now leave you all.

ADDRESS.

"HINTING AT FACTS."

BY A BOY.

I wanted my Teacher to give *me* a piece
    To speak on the Sunday-school stage—
But he being *tall* thought I was too small,
    And my services would not engage.

So I am left out of the Programme, you see,
    My name and *my* talents unknown!
He thought I might blunder, and make people wonder,
    But—I have a tongue of my own.

And now I will use it—Friends! listen and hear—
    'Tis Washington's birth-day you know,
When we may rejoice in our freedom of voice,
    And speak plainly to friend or to foe.

I don't like to be slighted, and kept out of sight,
    And I want my good teacher to hear it;
And others are here who have some things to fear
    If I proclaim the whole truth, or near it.

Here's our neighbor C*****—a very good man—
  Who promised a book-case to make us—
But some how or other that well-beloved brother
  Has managed thus far to forsake us!

Our school has a Banner, a beautiful one!
  I tell you, for fear you won't know it—
And when good brother W**** gets *his* promise done
  We'll have a large case made to show it.

And now for our Tickets—"twenty-five cents apiece!"
  For *myself*, I don't think them dear, sir!
But some lovers of "tin" thought the price was a sin,
  And *they* are a great way from here, sir!

Please tell them, my friends! we were "not to be beat,"
  Should absent ones deign to inquire—
That our Sabbath-school féte gave the people a treat,
  And I'll now take my seat—and retire.

ON AN INFANT.

Ay, loved one! to thy Maker go,
  Nor stay thee here to weep—
Earth's pleasures thou may'st well forego
  In Jesus' arms to sleep.

TO A SABBATH SCHOLAR.

KNEELING AT THE ALTAR OF PRAYER THE NIGHT BEFORE HIS DEPARTURE FOR SEA.

I saw thee at God's altar bend,
   And breathed a fervent prayer
That He who is the sinner's Friend
   Would bless thee kneeling there.
'Twas manly thus to take thy stand,
   To seek the Lord in youth—
To join the Saviour's praying band,
   And own the power of Truth.

My prayer, young man, shall follow thee
   When thou art far away—
May God protect thee on the sea,
   Mid dangers, night and day.
Oh! "seek and find" His promise sure,
   Thy heart to Jesus give—
Salvation through His blood secure,
   And you with Christ shall live.

OPENING ADDRESS.

FOR CHRISTMAS ANNIVERSARY.

BY A BOY.

Friends of the Sabbath-school:

I feel myself honored by my Teachers in being selected to deliver the Opening Address of our Anniversary, though I cannot divine the reason of their choice, unless it be to save "the best of the wine to the last of the feast." I see other members of the school, who have been longer connected with it, who might have done our teachers more credit as their first speaker—yet, as the duty is mine to perform, I will do the best I can, and leave to your kindness all my errors and imperfections.

We come to-night to make a renewed thankoffering to our Creator for the manifold mercies of the year—for the prosperity he has bestowed upon our Sabbath-school—for the kind friends he has given us—for the Bible and its precious promises—and for the hope we cherish of sharing in heaven the joys of the redeemed if we prove faithful to the end of our present life.

In the kind providence of our heavenly Father we are again permitted to celebrate the anniversary of the day which more than any other awakens the most pleasing reflections in the minds of the children of God. With it we associate the birth of our dear Saviour—the brightest and most cheering event in the history of the world. The advent of a Redeemer formed the burden of the earliest promise made to fallen man. It was remembered by Job, sweetly whispered by David, and gloriously foretold by Isaiah; and patriarchs and prophets, with earnest gaze, strained their eyes down the dim vista of ages and longed for the fulfillment of the promise. And at last, when Jesus *was* born in Bethlehem of Judea, angels in a rapture of delight flew with the glad tidings to man; the heavenly host shouted, "Glory to God in the highest—on earth peace and good will to man," and the eternal vaults of highest heaven resounded with the jubilee of exultant praises to "God and *the Lamb*."

Eighteen centuries have rolled away since then. The human race had been plunged in iniquitous darkness, and only here and there the light of a righteous character had glimmered faintly amid the dreary waste of sin. Now the rays of the Sun of Righteousness are fast penetrating the gloomy mists of idolatry ; its warming beams are softening the hard hearts of men—causing that which was once dead to become alive, and that which was once barren to become fruitful.

Again it is Christmas! With this morning's earliest dawn, angels and cherubim tuned their harps anew, and heaven is to-night harmonious with joyful anthems. Sweetly and triumphantly they are wafted over the fair fields of Paradise, till even the little stars above us seem to twinkle in melodious concert. At the time of so much rejoicing how becoming it is that the children of earth also should remember the day which witnessed the birth of Him "who was wounded for their transgressions and bruised for their iniquities!" Sorrowfully be it said there is not that unity among them that there is among the inhabitants of the better world. But the thousands and tens of thousands who have this day assembled in God's sanctuaries in our own as well as in other lands, and the multitudes of Sabbath-school children who crowd his altars to-night, all bear testimony of the efficacy of a Saviour's blood, and of the love which fills the heart of his people.

Again it is Christmas! Since we last greeted our friends and teachers here, God has granted to our

Sabbath-school a year of uninterrupted prosperity. In the world there have been reverses. Fortunes have been overthrown; blood has been spilled; lives have been lost, and many who but a short time ago were revelling in wealth and splendor, with bright anticipations of long life, are now destitute and penniless, or moldering in the soldier's grave. But while without there has been much of sorrow and disappointment, how different has it been with us! Fifty-two times have we met our kind teachers in the Sabbath-school and united with them in hymns of worship and praise. One hundred and four opening prayers have been offered up to our heavenly Father to make us—his children—wise and happy.— Our superintendent and teachers, remembering the living injunction of the dear Saviour, "Feed my Lambs," have labored faithfully for our good.— Freely have they distributed the bread of life, and many have been the seed they have sown. Though as yet, dear teachers, time hath revealed but few even of the germs, yet remember "ye shall reap if ye faint not." God will bless your efforts, and ye shall behold in the garner of eternity the fruits.— Gratefully we recall the many tender words you have spoken to us the last year, and the earnest admonitions with which you have warned us to be good and holy children ; and we truly feel that we LOVE you, dear teachers, and, above all, that God who gave us our birth in a land of Sabbath-schools, and who has blessed us with friends so solicitous for our welfare.

We have much to be thankful for. Yes, we should be thankful that "Death's doings" among our little band has been so limited. With few exceptions, we commence this New Year with the same number of young hearts and smiling faces as in 1864. And who are the exceptions? The eye of the stranger misses them not—but there *are* hearts bleeding here to-night who remember "the dear departed dead" who once rejoiced and mingled with us in our Sabbath-school Anniversaries. One was a devoted Teacher. She was true to her trust. Patient and mild in the discharge of her duties as a Teacher, she won the attention and affections of the children, and they will cherish her name and faithfulness and virtues till they too shall be called from the church militant to the church triumphant. Beside her aged mother, whose prayers and tears ye have all heard and seen who are familiar with the revivals in this church, this daughter is sleeping—and though the cold grave has received the form of our beloved Teacher, we are assured from God's Bible that it shall rise again—that "mortal shall put on immortality"—and come forth at the resurrection of the just in newness of strength and beauty.

> A grave-yard is a school to teach
>   The living how to live—
> And has a silent power to preach
>   Which pulpits cannot give.

And there was another, "who is not, for God took her." Three months have passed since we followed the beautiful remains of one of our former associates to the "place of tombs" near by *that* Teacher. Lucinda has also "escaped to the mansions of light." Often has she stood upon this Anniversary platform! Often has her voice been heard, like music's numbers, within these walls, in dialogues, recitations, and singing—when the gladness of her heart beamed in her face and gladness filled the hours. In the retrospect, I again see Lucinda! With eyes expressing tenderness—with a heart big with hope and full of sympathy—with a graceful, unassuming step, she lived and moved among us—a pleasant companion—an obedient child. But

> When last I saw her, oh! how changed! how pale!
>   The rose bloom from her pallid cheek had fled;
> With hasty steps she trod life's gloomy vale,
>   As fell consumption on her vitals prey'd.

And now she has gone! That gentle girl will take part in our exercises no more! The chord is broken at the fountain, and the wheel at the cistern. The spirit has fled that once animated that meek-eyed, lovely one. And whither has it fled? "I go to prepare mansions for you," said the Saviour to his followers, "that where I am there ye may be also." And who that once knew Lucinda can doubt that she followed Christ? While in health, she loved his name and loved his cause. You might "read of heaven and learn the way" from her daily walk. She loved her Saviour's friends—her Saviour's praying ones—and the testimony of her short life here, as shown in her acts, was always in favor of Religion and Piety. While racked with pain and emaciated with disease, she murmured not.— She was willing to suffer—"but had rather," she answered, "be absent from the body, to be present with the Lord." She thought "for her to depart and be with Christ, would be far better,"—yet, I heard her say, "Not my will, but thine be done."— When struck with Death—when the messenger of release had come—she told her mother she was "going to die *now*"—and then in an exulting tone, with her eyes raised in prayer, she exclaimed,—

"Now, dear Jesus, take me now." And she was dead.

We strewed fresh roses on her coffin-lid, as it was lowered into the earth, and there left Lucinda beside the little grave of another member who had died last year, to await the sounding of the trump that shall awake the dead and bid the sleepers rise.— Then we shall see them again, where thousands will meet who were on earth members of the Sabbath-school.

> "I want to put on my attire,
>   Washed white in the blood of the Lamb;
> I want to be one of that choir,
>   And tune my sweet harp to His name.
> I want—oh! I want to be there,
>   Where Sorrow and Sin bid adieu—
> Your joy and your friendship to share,
>   To wonder and worship with you."

EPITAPH ON A CHRISTIAN LADY.

Receive thy trust, O Grave! receive this sacred dust!
  Our mother here we bring awhile to thee—
But soon thy doors will ope, when Jesus calls the just,
  And she will rise, from thy dark prison free:
For she was Christ's—in Him she lived and died,
No other God she knew, and never Him denied;
A Christian's life she led—with daily praying breath
She filled her years on earth, and triumphed over death.

RECITATION.

THOUGHTS ON THE TIMES.

BY A BOY.

I wonder where the soldiers are
    That used to march and play,
When May and I, and ma and pa,
    Went walking on Broadway.
Their boots and buttons looked so new,
    Their swords and guns so bright!
And then they looked so pleasant too,
    I *could* not think they'd *fight!*

The other day I went again
    With Charley Smith and May,
And heard the men in Central Park
    On drums and trumpets play.
They sit so stiff and look so plain,
    And the music is so queer!
I wished I might go home again
    If no "soldier-boongs" were here.

Just then a poor man hobbled by;
  He seemed so pale and slim,
And looked so sadly from his eye,
  I almost cried for him.
One arm was gone, and there instead
  His coat sleeve dangled free—
He had a hank'chief 'round his head,
  And looked so kind at me.
I'm sure he had a little child
  He thought of, passing by,
And when he looked at me and smiled
  So sad, *I had to cry.*

And when I learned that this poor man
  Was the soldier of to-day,
And this the cause I never ran
  To see them march and play—
That all the rest were at the war
  To make it safe at home,
I raised my little heart to God
  And prayed, "Thy kingdom come!"

And then I thought when I grew up
  To keep a great big store,
That poor lame soldier should not work
  Nor ever want for more.

Aug. 29, '64.   Jr.

SUPPLEMENTARY
TO
MY SABBATH SCHOOL SCRAP BOOK,
Original and Select.

"There's a draught that heaven distilleth,
　Pure as crystal from the skies;
Freely, whosoever willeth,
　May partake it, and be wise."

DIALOGUE.

BY A BOY AND GIRL—AT A TABLE.

"THE OMNIBUS."

James. Good morning, Miss Wiggins. I've called to see you on very important business. I want your advice.

Mary. What's the matter, James? I hope you haven't got into any trouble.

J. Oh, yes; I'm in a peck of trouble, and I want you to help me out.

M. Me! to help you out; why how can I do it?

J. Easy enough. You know we're going to have an exhibition at our Sunday-school, and they want me to write a dialogue for the occasion, and I want you to help. I don't know what to write about, and you must help me out of the scrape.

M. Well, if that's all you want I can easily tell you what to write about. I'd write something good and sharp about long sermons, especially prosy ones.

J. But that wouldn't do—it wouldn't be apropos, and it might hurt the minister's feelings. You know ministers are very sensitive.

M. Then I'd give them a dialogue on good order in the school, and I'd make it pretty plain too.

J. I'm afraid that would be too common-place. I don't think I could make it lively enough, and then it might offend the Superintendent.

M. I wouldn't care for that—you can't expect to please everybody. But I'll tell you what would be better: write a piece on Sunday-school gossiping. I think you could make a coat out of that that would fit a good many.

J. That's very true, but I'm afraid it might be considered personal. You know Sunday-school gossiping is so common with us that it would hit most every one in our school.

M. Well, suppose it does, that's just what you want to do. How do you expect to correct the bad habits of people unless you show them up?

J. Can't you think of something else?

M. Well, you might write a piece about those hangers on who lounge about the sidewalk and in the lobby, staring decent people out of countenance. Call it the Sidewalk Member. That would be a good title.

J. That *would* be a good subject. But it would have to be made very pointed and severe to have any effect on those fellows. They're so abominably impudent that they never take a hint without a kick, and then they always want the kick first.

M. I really think you would be doing the Sunday-school a good service if you could only show these fellows up in the proper light. I think it's a scandalous practice—this hanging around the school staring at the young ladies and mimicking and ridiculing everything that's going on. It's a practice that no well-bred young man would be guilty of.

J. And that's just the reason why I think I couldn't be severe enough. If they were decently bred I could give them some hints that they couldn't fail to take. But as it is, I'm afraid it would be a fruitless task.

M. How would a dialogue on Sunday-school training and instruction do? You might have five or six characters in it to bring out the whole subject. That would be profitable as well as entertaining.

J. Worse and worse. It would never do in the world; they want something spicy and spirited, and at the same time appropriate. And that's what bothers me. If I write a plain, straight forward moral piece they'll call it "flat," "old fogy," "behind the age." You see I want to write a piece that will take. Something that will bring the "house down." This is a fast age, and nothing common-place will do.

M. I know it's a fast age, and that's just the reason why good, sound moral sentiment is more needed. And if I were you I wouldn't pander to a false, trashy taste. I'd write something substantial or I wouldn't write at all.

J. That's what I've called to see you about.— Now what shall it be?

M. Well, suppose you write an address instead of a dialogue. You could make it a sort of an omnibus, and include all these different things in it.

J. That's not a bad idea. Let's try (takes out paper and pencil). An omnibus—say for twelve passengers. Well, who shall the first be?

M. I think I'd let Mr. Long Sermon step in first. He's an old gentleman, and he'll want a good seat.

J. (writing*)* Very well, he shall have a good seat, and I'll hetchel him when I get him it.

M. Suppose you have the Sunday-school gossip for the next?

J. (writing) Put him down. No, put *her* down,

that's a "she." That branch of industry belongs to the ladies. Who next?

M. Not altogether, sir, if you please. I think the "*he's*" do their full share of it; so you may as well take one along with the "she."

J. (writing) Very well, then, have a "he" Sunday-school gossip and a she to match. What grand game they'll be. Who next?

M. I'd put the sidewalk member in next.

J. (writing) In he goes, and I'll give him a dose that will kill or cure. Who next?

M. Suppose you put in the "indoor lounger" next? I mean those fellows who seem to come to the Sunday school meetings without any particular object, except perhaps to warm themselves and pass away time.

J. And write in the hymn-books and stare at the young ladies. (Writing.) Down he goes. Who next?

M. Let Mr. Scandal step in next; you can make a good point on him.

J. (writing) "Miss Scandal" you mean. Every time I hear her name mentioned I think I feel a cat scratching at my back. (Scratches his back.)

M. Now how many have you got?

J. (reading) That makes six, and I'll have room for six more.

M. We'll put "Mr. Brag" in for one.

J. Oh, yes, and there's "Mr. Blower" too; "Brag and Blower," that's a great firm. They do a large business; but I think one of that firm will be enough. (Writing.) I'll put "Miss Flirt" in next. She's an amiable young lady, and I think she'd like to have a ride. (Writing.)

M. You might give the next seat to the Fop; he'll be good company on the journey.

J. (writing) Very well, and I'll put "The Miser" in next; he won't take up much room, and a good ride may do him good.

M. There's another character I wish you'd put in—the "Behind Time." He's always late at church, late at school, late at dinner, and late to bed. I think the country air may restore him.

J. I don't know about that. I think he's past recovery. But I'll try him. (Writing.) Now I've got just room for one more.

M. Well, give that seat to "Mr. Idler;" perhaps his fellow-passengers may improve him, though I think it's very doubtful. I am afraid he's a confirmed case. He's living to no purpose. He neither gets good nor does good.

J. (writing) That's true, but perhaps the example of "Miss Gossip" and "Mr. Brag" may keep him from stagnating. Now we're full, and what a company we've got!

M. A beautiful company indeed.

J. Wouldn't you like to go along, Miss Wiggins? I'll take you on top with me.

M. No, I thank you, not I. You don't catch me in such company. Are you going to drive?

J. To be sure I am. Do you think I'd trust such a precious load to any one else?

M. Then I've one request to make. I hope you'll drive that omnibus so fast and so far before you get back your passengers will be all metamorphosed into decent people.

EPITAPH.

We've laid our children down to sleep,
   In this sweet resting-place—
No longer will their parents weep,
For Jesus will these jewels keep
   While gone from our embrace.

DIALOGUE.

JOHN AND WILLIAM'S CHOICE.

BY MOTHER AND SONS.

JOHN.

I MEAN to be a soldier,
   With uniform quite new;
I wish they'd let me have a drum,
   And be a captain too:
I would get amid the battle,
   With a broadsword in my hand,
And hear the cannon rattle,
   And the music all so grand.

MOTHER.

My son, my son!—what if that sword
   Should strike a noble heart,
And bid some loving father
   From his little ones depart?
What comfort would your waving plumes
   And brilliant dress bestow,
When you thought upon his widow's tears
   And her orphan's cry of woe?

WILLIAM.

I mean to be a President,
    And rule each rising state,
And hold my levees once a week,
    For all the gay and great.
I'll be a king, except the crown,—
    But that they won't allow;
And I'll find out what the tariff is,
    That puzzles me so now.

MOTHER.

My son, my son! the cares of state
    Are thorns upon the breast,
That ever pierce the good man's heart,
    And rob him of his rest.
The great and gay to him appear
    As trifling as the dust;
For he knows how little they are worth,—
    How faithless of their trust.

RECITATION.

LITTLE ROBERT REED'S RESOLUTION.

"I'll never use tobacco, no;
    It is a filthy weed;
I'll never put it in my mouth,"
    Said little Robert Reed.

"Why, there was idle Jessie Jones,
　　As dirty as a pig;
　He smoked when only ten years old,
　　And thought it made him big.

"He spent his time and money, too,
　　And made his mother sad;
　She feared a worthless man would come
　　Of such a worthless lad.

"Oh, no, I'll never smoke or chew;
　　'Tis very wrong indeed;
　It hurts the health, it makes bad breath,"
　　Said little Robert Reed.

RECITATION.

THE HOUSEMAID'S SOLILOQUY.

To be spoken by a large Girl, dressed in the costume of a housemaid, using a broom or duster.

1. Oh, dear, dear! Wonder if my mistress *ever* thinks I am made of flesh and blood? Five times, within half an hour, I have trotted up stairs, to hand her things, that were only four feet from her rocking-chair. Then, there's her son, Mr. George,

—it does seem to me that a great able-bodied man like him, needn't call a poor tired woman up four pair of stairs to ask, "what's the time of day?"— Heigh ho!—it's "Sally do this," and "Sally do that!" till I wish I never had been named at all; and I might as well go farther back, while I am about it, and wish I had never been born.

2. Now, instead of ordering me round so like a dray-horse, if they would only look up smiling-like, now and then; or ask me how my "rheumatiz" did, or say, "Good morning, Sally;" or show some sort of interest in a fellow-creature, I could pluck up a bit of heart to work for them. A kind word would ease the wheels of my tread-mill amazingly, and wouldn't cost *them* anything, either.

3. Look at my clothes, all at sixes and sevens! I can't get a minute to sew on a string or a button, except at night; and then I am so sleepy it is as much as ever I can find the way to bed; and what a bed it is, to be sure! Why even the pigs are now and then allowed clean straw to sleep on; and as to bed-clothes, the less said about them the better; my old cloak serves for a blanket, and the sheets are as thin as a charity-school soup.

4. Well, well; one wouldn't think it, to see all the fine, glittering things down in the drawing-

room,—Miss Clara's diamond ear-rings, and mistress' rich dresses. I try to think it is all right; but it's no use

5. To-morrow's Sunday—" day of rest," I believe they call it. Humph ! more cooking to be done—more company—more confusion than on any other day in the week. If I own a soul, I haven't heard how to take care of it for many a long day. Wonder if my master and mistress calculate to pay me for *that*, if I lose it ? It is a *question* in my mind. Land of Goshen ! I ain't sure I've got a mind. [*bell rings.*] There's the bell again.   FERN.

THE AMERICAN BOY.

BY FATHER AND SON.

"FATHER, look up, and see that flag,
  How gracefully it flies;
Those pretty stripes—that seem to be
  A rainbow in the skies."

It is your country's flag, my son,
  And proudly drinks the light,
O'er ocean's wave—in foreign climes,
  A symbol of our might.

THE AMERICAN BOY.

"Father, what fearful noise is that,
    Like thundering of the clouds?
Why do the people wave their hats,
    And rush along in crowds?"

It is the noise of cannonry,
    The glad shouts of the free;
This is a day to memory dear—
    'Tis Freedom's Jubilee.

"I wish that I was now a man,
    I'd fire my cannon too,
And cheer as loudly as the rest—
    But, father, why don't you?"

I'm getting old and weak—but still
    My heart is big with joy;
I've witnessed many a day like this,
    Shout you aloud, my boy.

"Hurrah! for Freedom's Jubilee!
    God bless our native land!
And may I live to hold the sword
    Of Freedom in my hand!"

Well done, my boy—grow up and love
    The land that gave you birth:
A home where Freedom loves to dwell,
    Is paradise on earth!

DIALOGUE.

BY TWO BOYS.

THE GOSPEL SHIP.

James. Hallo, shipmate, I think I know you, and if I am not mistaken your name is John Faithful, and the last I heard of you, you had shipped on board of the old ship Methodism, which was at that time commanded by Jesus Christ of Nazareth.

John. You are not mistaken, (gives his hand,) I am the same man, and am still engaged on board the same ship, and I expect to stay during life, and we have the same Captain—a better never was.

James. But I should think that the old craft begins to be scarcely seaworthy from old age; and as there has been great improvements in ship building since she was built, I should think that you would like to take a chance at something new.

John. It is true she is somewhat old; I believe she was first sent to sea about one hundred years ago, but I think she is none the worse for that ;— she is built of excellent materials, her timbers will never rot, and she is planked with Salvation quite down to the keel ; so that the tooth of time, and the sea-worm together cannot make a scratch upon her.

James. Where was she built ? who gave her draft and prepared her mould ? and who were the workmen ?

John. I understand that she was launched from the old Foundry Dock in London ; her plan, or draft, was conceived in the eternal Mind, and Divine Providence gave out the moulds, piece by piece ; she was built by Messrs. John and Charles Wesley & Co., and they had some first-rate men to labor with them. When she was ready for sea, she was greater and better than either John or Charles thought she would be.

James. When she was first sent out, if I recollect, she was considered as an opposition to the old established line, and many things were said against her.

John. Yes, there was a wonderful hue and cry raised against her, and every one that went on board of her ; but as to her being an opposition to the true old line, *that* she never was ; she was considered safer, and in some cases faster than the old established line; she carried cheaper and the fare was better, consequently she did the best business; the poor as well as the rich could always find good berths on board of her.

James. I thought when I saw her bow that it did not look well; I did not admire the figure-head—it was the representation of a Lamb that had been slain, and it was covered with blood, and the pendant which was flying looked dismal to me; it was the sign of the Cross, and on it also were marks of blood.

John. When she is at a distance, she does not look well, but the more you examine her, the better she appears; and as to the figure-head, we think it most admirable; the Lamb there is the Lamb of God, that taketh away the sin of the world; and as you said it was covered with blood, that is the blood of Christ which cleanseth from all sin; and the pendant with the Cross and stained with blood, declares to all, that we depend upon the merit of Christ crucified, for salvation, and I can assure you, James, that it is a first-rate dependence in hard weather.

James. But I assure you, John, that I did admire her sails and rigging; I thought from her appearance, that she could use every breeze to advantage, but some of her sails I did not understand, as I never had seen them on any other ship.

John. Well, my good fellow, I see you are awake to nautical equipage; you soon discovered, as you thought, we had something new about us; but in reality they are not new, only rigged in a little different form. That small sail forward that is carried by old Methodism, which we call Class-meetings, was found on the old ship Apostolic, and also on the old Prophetic, but was not then called by the same name; and another, which seems to you to be new, is what we call Love Feasts, and when carried on the Apostolic, were called Feasts of Charity. The other sails are more common, but some of them so formed and rigged, that they work quicker and to better effect than on any other vessel I have ever seen.

James. I admired the anchors very much, they seemed to me to be as they ought—but there was something written upon the stocks of them, which I could not read or understand.

John. Well, James, that is all very plain to me; it is a good hope through grace of everlasting life, which hope is sure and steadfast.

James. I did not have an opportunity of examining her cables; are they hemp or chain?

John. Neither hemp or chain, but stronger than either; they are faith; that faith which is of the operation of the Spirit of God, and is always bright if well taken care of; these cables neither rot, rust, or break, and they are long; they reach to that within the vale, which the forerunner, Jesus Christ, for us hath entered.

James. I should like to know how she stands hard weather and severe gales; did you ever see her in a severe storm?

John. I can assure you she is first-rate in a storm; she has passed a number that I can call to mind, and I think she can stand as many more. There was a tremendous storm in the year 1765, in and about the latitude of London, when Mr. Maxfield, Mr. Bell, and about six hundred with them, left her for fear that they were following a wrong course.—Another took her off the coast of Maryland, when Mr. O'Kelly and his party jumped overboard, determined to build a ship for themselves, but in this they failed. She has encountered something of the same kind in and about the latitude of New York, but in every case she has rode majestically upon the boisterous waves, astonishing all but her Captain and great Architect—and I think myself perfectly safe on board of her.

James. How is the fare you get, the work you do, and the pay?

John. The fare is first-rate, and we have fresh bread every day; no stale bread on board of her; fresh manna every morning, noon and night, and water fresh from the well of Salvation, and often some of the wine of the Kingdom. The key of the storeroom is given to every one, and if they will use it, they will always have plenty, but they that are unwilling to work, often complain that they are hungry and thirsty, and although often spoken to by the Captain, and urged to work by his officers, yet some of them go on complaining. The pay seems to be as much as you are willing to draw; we receive checks on the bank of heaven, already signed, and we are allowed to fix upon them the amount, and they are always honored and never refused; for our Captain is well known in heaven, and after the voyage is over, we are to have palms of victory and crowns of glory, and be made kings and priests forever. The work is not hard; she is well manned, and every one is designated to work; her rigging works easy, and when we all pull together to the song of the Leader, all goes well, and the work is very pleasant.

James. I should like to hear the song by which you pull.

John. The old song is very pleasant to me; I will try and sing it.

>The everlasting gospel
> Has launched the deep at last,
>Behold her sails suspended
> Around her towering mast.
>Around her decks in order
> The joyful sailors stand,
>Crying, O! here we go
> To Immanuel's happy land.
>
>We're now on the wide ocean,
> We bid the earth farewell;
>But where we shall cast anchor
> No mortal tongue can tell.
>About our future happiness
> There need be no debate,
>While we ride on the tide
> With our Captain and his mate.
>
>We're passengers united
> In harmony and love;
>The wind's all in our favor,
> How joyfully we move!
>Though troubles may surround us
> And raging billows roar,
>We will sweep through the deep
> Till we land on Canaan's shore.

DIALOGUE.

"HAPPY NEW YEAR."

BY TWO GIRLS.

Caroline. What do you think, sister Margaret! I hav'nt heard a single boy or girl wish our friends here a happy New Year yet! Isn't it strange?

Margaret. Yes, 'tis a little strange—but, sister, how did you happen to think of it now? I guess you have just woke up, hav'nt you?

Caroline. Bless you, no, Margaret,—but isn't it the custom? and one, too, "as old as the hills?" And shouldn't custom be followed? Why, I've heard bigger folks than we wish happy New Year to-day!

Margaret. I know it is the custom, sister,—and being the custom, the wish you speak of is frequently uttered without sincerity. I have no doubt thousands of children have this day said, "happy New Year," without understanding its meaning.— And can you tell me, sister, what it means?

Caroline. I think I can, Margaret. When I wished mother "happy New Year," this morning, I meant her to give me something.

Margaret. There now, I thought so. And perhaps that's what you mean by wishing "happy New Year" to-night! What I mean by "happy New Year," is, that our friends may enjoy peace, happiness and prosperity during the New Year.

Caroline. Well, Margaret, I hope they may—but shouldn't they give us something for our good wishes? I believe if the children should, with one voice, wish "happy New Year," the people couldn't help *hearing* it, and would certainly make an extra present to our school. Suppose we try it, Margaret.

Margaret. If it would do any good, I should have no objection. But I think it will prove a "great cry and little wool"—therefore, let us make the wish in behalf of the children, and if the friends feel disposed to assist our school, well and good.

Caroline. No, no, Margaret—let us all join in,—and if it doesn't bring the pennies, we'll make less noise next time. Now, children, are you ready?

"HAPPY NEW YEAR!"

R.

RECITATION.

THE CLOSING YEAR

BY A GIRL.

The year has past along, and brings
    Us nearer death's cold shore;
Yet still earth's vain and trifling things
    Charm as they did of yore.

The closing year! What solemn reflections it ought to inspire in our bosoms! We live in a Christian country, where, if we please, we may enjoy the richest blessings; but alas! how many of us trample the laws of our God beneath our feet! how many of us, by our crimes, wickedness or faults, crucify our Redeemer, and open his wounds afresh! Let us strive never to do so again; let us pray for grace that we may be found walking in the laws and ordinances of the Lord blameless.

But little real happiness is to be found below. How many began the last year with the proudest anticipations of happiness, and have had their hopes blighted! How many expect perfect happiness in the present! Some author says,

> "For scarcely have we entered,
>   New year! thy courts with glee;
> Yet many a heart has centered
>   Its brightest hopes in thee."

As all earthly hopes are frequently blighted, let not our expectations be confined to earth; but let our fondest, our most glorious anticipations be of Heaven—that bright, that angelic country, where sorrow and want can never enter; where all is celestial, effulgent light, love ineffable, and glory unspeakable!

> Could I but go at once to God,
>   How happy should I be!
> But I must tread life's thorny road,
>   No perfect bliss for me!
> Yet should I die and go to Heaven,
>   Glory would round me shine;
> My sins they all would be forgiven;
>   Whose glory like to mine?

But another year is rising before us. We may, in this year, advance in temporal and spiritual concerns; so that it may be said of us, that "we are Israelites indeed, in whom there is no guile." The goodness of God invites us to approach him, and give him our confidence, our love, our all. It has been said, and truly,

> "The earth affords no lovelier sight
> Than a religious youth."

Oh that we all might be religious; that all the earth would not only believe in God, but also obey him! Alas! although nearly all believe in him, few illustrate the doctrines they profess, by their actions. Their religion is of the understanding, not of the heart. Many begin the new year with new resolutions; but how few, comparatively, have strength to keep them! God is great, but he is also good; he will give to them who ask him, strength to keep their good resolutions, and to abandon their bad ones.

RECITATION.

BY AN INFANT SCHOLAR.

Though I am but a little boy,
I would my youthful mind employ
In striving knowledge to obtain,
And not spend all my days in vain.

Although my prospects are not bright,
Yet I am not discouraged quite :
For of great Franklin 'tis related,
That his young mind was cultivated,
Whereby he rose to wealth and fame,
With L. L. D. join'd to his name.

And I have somewhere seen it stated,
And never knew the fact debated,
That Isaac Newton, Socrates,
Mark Tully, and Demosthenes,
Were once quite tiny boys like me,
And scarce had done with A, B, C,
But yet by dint of application,
They rose to seats of elevation ;
And by their oratoric thunder
Fill'd Rome, and half the world with wonder.

And may'nt a boy of mod'rate talents,
Observing strict and even balance,
By rigid, patient application,
Hope to attain some useful station,
And strew some benefits around,—
Nor be a cumberer of the ground?
But lest your patience be expended,
My crude oration must be ended.
My thanks to you, respected Teacher,
For list'ning to so dull a preacher.

DIALOGUE.

BY TWO GIRLS.

THE SUNDAY SCHOOL SHIELD.

Lucinda. Well, Margaret, how do you like the Sunday-school?

Margaret. Exceedingly well, I regard it as the Shield of the Youth.

Lucinda. The Shield of the Youth, Margaret? why how can that be? I thought a Shield was a broad piece of defensive armor, worn on the left arm, or held in the left hand, to ward off assaults made by the foe.

Margaret. Yes, Lucinda, so it is; but do you not know that almost every word in the English language admits of various significations, and that by a figure of speech any thing that serves to protect is called a Shield?

Lucinda. True, Margaret; but then how does the Sunday-school serve as a protector?

Margaret. Well, Lucinda, I will tell you: in the first place, every child brought into the school is taken from the exposure to vice that otherwise would be continually before it; and in the second place, it is brought under the influence of the good example of the virtuous and pious part of the community, and is thus shielded from vice. For this reason, I call the Sunday-school a Shield to the Youth.

Lucinda. Really, Margaret, you reason well. I had not thought of this before; I had thought the Sunday school only designed for poor children, to teach such as would not have an opportunity, otherwise, to obtain an education.

Margaret. Ah! true, this was the object originally; but the experiment was so signally owned and blessed of God, in a moral point of view, that for many years this institution has been regarded as the hand-maid of religion, and the most efficient auxiliary of the church; and I have often felt astonished at the indifference manifested in the church to the interest of the Sunday-school. I wonder that Christians, and especially Christian parents, so seldom visit it.

Lucinda. Well, Margaret, I must confess that I had but a very poor opinion of the Sunday-school before; I thought it a mere show of benevolence, a confinement for the children, and a heavy tax upon the teachers and friends of the cause; but now I see it differently, and I wish you would tell me how it may be promoted.

Margaret. Yes, Lucinda, I will, with all my heart; in the first place, we need teachers in the School, and, in the second place, there are many children in the streets that need to be brought into the school. This may be done by visitors going out and seeking them, and bringing them in; there is plenty of work for every member of the church, and every one of them may be profitably employed in this work.

Lucinda. Oh, Margaret, I see—I see now—oh, how strange it is that I have not known before the benefits of this institution, and been employed in it; but now I must try to make up lost time, and I will begin now, and here, for I perceive I have a good opportunity.

Dear friends, I want your attention to this subject. I discover that it is one of interest to us all. Christian friends ! can you be better employed than in the interest of the Sunday-school? Here your neighbors—your friends—your children may be instructed in virtue—the grace which alone can fit them for good society here, and Heaven and glory hereafter.

Parents, will you lend a helping hand? Will you become teachers or visitors? Young men and young women, will you come to the support of the school, and try to save the children from folly and vice? Will you take us by the hand and guide us in the path of virtue? Can you see little children thronging the road to death, and not run to our relief? Come, re-engage—save us, or we perish?

MY BIBLE.

"Within this awful volume lies
The mystery of mysteries;
Happiest they of human race
To whom their God has given grace
To read, to fear, to hope, to pray,
To lift the latch, to force the way;
And better they had ne'er been born
Who read to doubt, or read to scorn."

ECHO.

EGO* AND ECHO.

[A good effect will be produced by using this piece as a dialogue. The speaker that personates the Echo, should be screened from the audience, and utter his part with the same tone of voice as the first speaker, though somewhat weaker.]

I ASKED of Echo, t'other day,
  (Whose words are few and often funny,)
What to a novice she could say
  Of courtship, love, and matrimony?
      Echo—" Matter-o'-money!"

Whom should I marry?—should it be
  A dashing damsel, gay and pert,—
A pattern of inconsistency;
  Or selfish, mercenary flirt?
      Echo—" Nary flirt!"

What if,—a-weary of the strife
  That long has lured the gay deceiver,—

---

* A Latin pronoun, signifying *I, myself.*

She promised to amend her life,
   And sing no more, can I believe her?
      Echo—" Leave her!"

But, if some maiden with a heart,
   On me should venture to bestow it;
Pray, should I act the wiser part
   To take the treasure, or forego it?
      Echo—" Go it!"

But, what if, seemingly afraid
   To bind her fate in Hymen's fetter,
She vows she means to die a maid,—
   In answer to my loving letter?
      Echo—" Let her!"

What if, in spite of her disdain,
   I find my heart entwined about
With Cupid's dear, delicious chain,
   So closely that I can't get out?
      Echo—" Get out!"

But, if some maid with beauty blest,
   And pure and fair as Heaven can make her,
Will share my labor and my rest,
   Till envious death shall overtake her?
      Echo—" Take her!"

JOHN G. SAXE.

DIALOGUE.

BETWEEN A WESTERN HUNTER* AND AN ATHEIST.

BY TWO BOYS.

Hunter. I say, stranger, what's that 'ere thing you've got in your hand, that looks so speckled like?

Reasoner. This? It's the "Free Inquirer."

H. The what? I tell you what, Mister, you needn't think to throw your flings out that way at a fellow. I asked you a civil question, and you needn't to name a fellow a free inquirer for it. We are used to making free in our country.

R. You are mistaken in my meaning. It was this paper I called the "Free Inquirer"—not you.

H. Hay? that thing? What do you call it? a paper and free inquirer, too! Now if that ain't funny, I don't know.

R. I see you do not understand me, and I must explain. This thin white sheet is called paper—

*May be spoken in character.

feel it. These black marks are letters printed on it, and we read the words that they make when they are put together.

H. Read! O, I mind now; mammy used to tell us that in the settlements people went to school and larnt to read; and she said how daddy and her couldn't read; that was the reason they didn't take any books with 'em when they moved out on to the range. But I never heard about newspapers and free inquirers.

R. This is a book. (Showing one.) See—'tis made of paper like this; and then it is folded up and bound between pasteboards and covered with leather so as to keep it safe.

H. Well, now, stranger, since I find you didn't mean to make fun of a body, I hope you won't take any *pride* in what I said; and I'd like to know more about that paper, as you call it. What is it for?

R. It's a newspaper published in New York to expose the superstitious notions about religion.

H. How does it do that?

R. Why, it comes right out and says that all religion is nonsense, and religious people are all fools and hypocrites.

H. I don't understand that somehow. There was John Davis that used to be a roarer to fight and get drunk and swear and play cards; and he went away off to camp-meeting and got religious; and ever since then he's been the civilest, best-behaved, honestest fellow all about. I reckon if you were to hear him talk you'd think so.

R. Psha! it is all delusion—all a pack of nonsense, I tell you.

H. Well, now, I'd like you to tell me what made him leave off his old capers all of a sudden.

R. The fellow got frightened by their screaming and shouting.

H. I don't think so. He's not so easy frightened, though he won't fight now; but I seed him one day in a fix that I reckon you wouldn't like to have been in. Everybody else seemed scared but him, and he wasn't more afraid than you are now.

R. Ah, yes! I know they have courage enough about common things, but they are afraid of the devil, and hell, and all that.

H. Why, stranger! see here now—ain't you afraid of the devil?

R. I!—nonsense—there is no devil.

H. Hay? no devil! How do you know?

R. How? Did you ever see the devil?

H. No; but I never seed everything.

R. Did you ever see anybody that had seen him?

H. No. But John Davis says there is a devil.

R. John Davis is a fool, and all his nonsense is a pack of lies.

H. Hallo, stranger, you'd better not call John Davis a fool. I tell you he ain't a fool, and he'd lick you in a minute—that is, if he'd fight. But he's a clever fellow anyhow, and I won't hear him abused behind his back.

R. I did not mean to abuse him. You must not mind such expressions. I only want to convince you of the folly of religion.

H. Well, then, you may go on—I begin to feel anxious to know how you found out it was all a pack of lies.

R. If you read the "Free Inquirer" you'll see.

H. Why, does that say so? How does that know?

R. Why, Mr. Owens, and Miss Wright, and Mr. Jennings carry on the paper, and they go on to prove that there is no God; and so religion can't be true because it pretends to be minding the word of God.

H. No God! no hell! no devil! May be I won't have a frolic. Why, then a body can get drunk, swear, and fight, and if he should kill a fellow it would be no great matter. But, stop. How do they know? I don't like to be cheated.

R. Why, they say it's just a superstitious notion the people have. Nobody ever saw God; and people can't be expected to believe contrary to the evidence of their own senses.

H. No, to be sure. But then John Davis says how that God made the world. If there ain't no God, who did make the world?

R. Make the world, indeed; how do you suppose he'd go about to make the world?

H. I don't know anything about it. I asked you to tell me how the world come if God didn't make it.

R. Come! it didn't come—it always was.

H. How do you know that?

R. Why, reason teachers us so. If there warn't something always, how could anything ever happen to be?

H. That's what I don't know. And I'll tell you another thing I don't know. If this world always was without any maker, did it make itself?

R. Make itself! Ha, ha, that's a good one!— Why, don't you know that the earth is dead matter? It couldn't make itself nor anything else.

H. Well, so I should judge; and if it couldn't make anything because it ain't alive, I wonder how it could change so much. The water runs—trees grows, leaves falls, and put out again—fire burns up a heap of truck—creatures, and birds, and fishes, and mankind, too, lives and dies, and nobody makes 'em. I can't understand that. They didn't always be, I know.

R. That's only the fortuitous concurrence of circumstances.

H. The what?

R. Why, its—its—it just happens so.

H. It's a queer sort of fixen, anyhow. I wonder if such things as this here rifle ever just happened so, without being made. Where did you say that 'ere free inquirer come from?

R. From New York.

H. Who did you say made it?

R. Mr. Owen—Miss Wright—and Mr. Jennings write the pieces in it, and then get the printers to print them.

H. What is printing? How is it done?

R. They have the letters cut on little pieces of lead (made hard somehow), these they call types; and they pick them up letter by letter, and put them in order so as to make words, and so on till they get all these letters set up to make one side; then they put them on a flat stone in the printing office, and black the types, and lay the paper on, and press them—and it looks like this side. Then they put up the same types in a different order, to make different words, and print the other side.

H. What do you call a letter? Let me see.

R. These are large letters at the top. Those small things are all letters.

H. And do they pick them up one by one, and fix 'em so as to make the whole paper?

R. Yes.

H. Now, Mister, I want to ask you a few questions. Did you ever see New York?

R. No; I am a Western man.

H. Did you ever see that woman and them men you talk about?

R. Who? Miss Wright, and Mr. Owen, and Mr. Jennings? No.

H. Did you see the folks make that paper and print it?

R. No, I tell you.

H. How do you know they did it then?

R. Can't I read? It says so.

H. Maybe it lies. How do you know it don't lie?

R. How do I know it don't lie? I know it don't. Do you think I am a fool?

H. If you ain't you can tell what I ask you.—It's a plain question. How do you know there is such a place as New York?

R. Why! the fellow's crazy. How do I know there are such people as Miss Wright, and Mr. Owen, and Mr. Jennings, when I've heard so much about them, and see their writings every week.—Can't I believe my eyes?

H. Yes; but that's the thing I want to know. How can you prove that they did write them things? To come right out, how can you prove that that paper was printed?

R. Why, I know it was. It couldn't make itself.

H. Yes, I know that, but then couldn't it grow so?

R. A newspaper grow! What nonsense! I read about printing, and this is what they make by printing.

H. As far as I can see, you don't know but what it grow'd. But couldn't it happen so?

R. Happen? No. What an absurd idea! It was made.

H. I don't see but it might *happen* without

being made, as easy as all this world anyhow. So now, good by, Mister! Wife is waiting for me, and I must go. But next time I see you, don't call John Davis a fool, or you and the hunter will have a fight. Do you hear that, old fellow?

THE SUNDAY-SCHOOL.

Behold the groups that cluster there!
Children within the place of prayer.
Think of the future harvest's power,
Whose seed is planted in this hour,—
The BIBLE, LIBRARY-BOOK, the word
Of love, by which the heart is stirred;—
The many precepts, kindly given,
The many hopes that dews of heaven
May fall, refreshing, on the soil,
And crown, with large increase, the toil.
Think of the mass of mind thus trained,
And say, is not a victory gained
O'er Error, Bigotry, and Sin?
With arms like these, shall we not win?
Think too, of those who, from their class,
As pupils, have been called to pass
To higher seats, where wisdom dwells,—
To pastures, where the cool deep wells
Of living waters gush, and He,
The Shepherd, dwells eternally?

RECITATION.

THE LAND OF THE BLEST.

BY FATHER AND SON.

"Dear father, I ask for my mother in vain;
Has she sought some far country, her health to regain?
Has she left our cold climate of frost and of snow,
For some warm, sunny land, where the soft breezes blow?"

"Yes, yes, gentle boy, thy loved mother is gone
To a climate where sorrow and pain are unknown;
Her spirit is strengthened, her frame is at rest;
There is health, there is peace, in the Land of the Blest."

"Is that land, my dear father, more lovely than ours?
Are the rivers more clear, and more blooming the flowers?
Does summer shine over it, all the year long?
Is it cheered by the glad sounds of music and song?"

"Yes, the flowers are despoiled not by winter or night;
The well-springs of life are exhaustless and bright;
And by exquisite voices sweet hymns are addressed
To the Lord who reigns over the Land of the Blest."

"Yet that land to my mother will lonely appear;
She shrunk from the glance of a stranger while here;
From her foreign companions I know she will flee,
And sigh, dearest father, for you and for me."

"My darling, thy mother rejoices to gaze
On the long-sever'd friends of her earlier days;
Her parents have there found a mansion of rest,
And they welcome their child to the Land of the Blest."

"How I long to partake of such meetings of bliss!
That land must be surely more happy than this;
On you, my kind father, the journey depends;
Let us go to my mother, her kindred, and friends."

"Not on me, love; I trust I may reach that bright clime,
But in patience I stay till the Lord's chosen time;
And must strive while awaiting his gracious behest,
To guide thy young steps to the Land of the Blest.

Thou must toil through a world full of dangers, my boy;
Thy peace it may blight, and thy virtues destroy;
Nor wilt thou, alas! be withheld from its snares
By a mother's kind counsels, a mother's fond prayers;

Yet fear not— the God, whose direction we crave,
Is mighty to strengthen, to shield, and to save;
And his hand may yet lead thee, a glorified guest,
To the home of thy mother, the Land of the Blest."

ADDRESS.

BY A BOY.

YOUNG AMERICA.

Ladies and Gentlemen :—We wish to-day to give you an introduction to Young America, Uncle Sam's pet boys—and trust that, if you consider them good-looking, you will receive them with favor, and give them encouragement.

We do not profess to be that particular nice kind of Uncle Sam's children that perambulate the streets in long-tailed coats, with long canes, puffing long cigars, swearing such long oaths, and sporting such splendid gold watches and mustaches. Neither do we claim relationship with those gents who are so eager for a muss, who talk such barbarous slang phrases, and "travel wid der macheen when she takes a run"—who are not above disturbing churches and peaceful congregations, making the night air sound hideous with their shouts. No, indeed, we do not spell in the same class with these Bulls and

Bears who are trying to slide in as Uncle Sam's younger children. The old gentleman says they may as well stop knocking, for they can't come in. Now you may not all of you have seen the old fellow, but he is alive and kicking for all that.

We are not afraid to present a bold and fearless front before the world. We sail under no false colors. We are for freedom in every shape. We shun the slavery of vice and habit as being as oppressive as the yoke of despotism. Like those beautiful colors in our National standard—the White, the Red, the Blue—that neither fade nor run, so we can look heavenward to-day and shout— " Where Liberty dwells there is my home."

We love to cheer the desponding, to raise the fallen, to dry the orphan's tear, and pour the balm of consolation into the stricken widow's heart, in the exercise of that active benevolence that does not let the right hand know what the left hand doeth.

Young America may sometimes be somewhat impetuous, and occasionally a little too much in haste. He judges that it is better far to err in advancing a good cause than to be found guilty of a mean action. He never says "I can't," when he can say "I'll try" so much better ; and prefers the railroad car of progress to the old fogy coach of conservativeness. Taking as his motto "Excelsior," he will be found pressing his way onward, upward, higher!

Young America loves the ladies. That you all know. Children will copy after their parents.— Young America loves his dear old mother as he loves his life. He sees in her the personification of every grace of character. Love, Virtue, Purity, Gentleness and Goodness in her shine out in all their perfection. He looks upon every female as under his protection, and never will stand by unmoved and hear modesty slandered or see innocence trampled upon. No—he spurns the wretch who would dare to lift his hand against or wag his tongue to sully the reputation of the gentle ones that look to man as their natural protector, clinging to him for support as the delicate twining ivy embraces the sturdy oak for succor against the bitter blasts of winter. In their cause the American boy becomes right valiant, and often proves that he can *act* as well as make fine speeches. And as he loves his mother, so he loves that dear "old family Bible that lays on the stand," from which his father used so often to read to him, and whose inspired truths teach him the way to heaven. Regarding this precious volume as the very keystone of that glorious arch of liberty upon which the free government of his country rests, and the basis of all its good laws, he means that it never shall be a proscribed book ; but all who will may read and learn, whether in public schoo')r anywhere else.

'Tis true that these young chaps like the smell of gunpowder sometimes, especially on the Fourth of July, the anniversary of his nation's freedom ; and while he looks up to the beautiful Stars and Stripes floating in the breeze over his head, and learns from his country's history what it cost his forefathers to enable them to hoist that proud ensign of liberty— while he reads the story of Bunker Hill, White Plains, Fort Greene, Trenton, Princeton, Saratoga, and Yorktown, his heart swells with gratitude to his Maker that there was ever such men as a Washington, Jefferson, Franklin, Adams, Jackson, and their gallant compeers, who could grapple with Tyranny and conquer it, and thus secure their nation's freedom. He remembers the beautiful sentiment of that noble Congress of 1776, who said to all the world : " We have counted the cost of this contest, and have with one mind resolved to die freemen rather than live slaves." While he also reads of Cerra Gorda, Monterey, Buena Vista, Vera Cruz, and Chapultepec, the glorious career of a Taylor and a Scott, and their honored aids — he remembers that now as well as then we must watch ever with jealous eye our social, civil and religious liberties to protect them from the insidious wiles of a foreign foe.

While we know that we have got to spend our twenty-one years and more in learning the value of a freeman's vote, we do not like that our Uncle's relations over the "big pond" should get ahead of us, in this respect, when they come to stay among us.

We would like to see our Uncle's watchword—"Liberty to all"—as the motto of every nation on the earth. And while pointing with just pride to our bright galaxy of thirty-six brilliant stars as individual evidences of the genius of the American people, we consider "Uncle Sam is rich enough to give us all a farm."

We can't go any more into particulars just now; but will just add, that while we have (got) the longest railroads, rivers, and canals; the tallest mountains and cataracts; the greatest telegraphs; the fastest steamships and yachts; the fattest babies, and the prettiest sisters and sweethearts of any nation on the globe—we mean to keep pushing ahead—considering, without further allegation, we have figured to a demonstration, that the universal Yankee Nation is the greatest one in all creation.

E. H. R.

RECITATION.

BY AN INFANT SCHOLAR.

I love this world so beautiful,
   I love the flowers and trees;
I love the softly murmuring brook,
   I love the cooling breeze.

I love the birds that sing so sweet,
   I love the gentle shower;
I love the little twinkling star,
   I love the twilight hour.

I love my Saviour best of all,
   I love to sing his praise;
I love to listen to His call:
   "Ye children, seek my grace."

I love to hear of Heaven, my home,
   Where all is bright and fair;
I love to think the time will come
   When I may enter there.

RECITATION.

WHAT IS THAT, MOTHER?

BY MOTHER AND CHILD.

What is that, Mother?
                The *Lark*, my child—
The morn has but just looked out, and smiled,
When he starts from his humble, grassy nest,
And is up and away, with the dew on his breast,
And a hymn in his heart, to yon pure, bright sphere,
To warble it out in his Maker's ear.
Ever, my child, be thy morn's first lays
Tuned, like the lark's, to thy Maker's praise.

What is that, Mother?
                The *Dove*, my daughter—
And that low, sweet voice, like a widow's moan,
Is flowing out from her gentle breast
Constant and pure by that lonely nest,
As the wave is poured from some crystal urn
For her distant dear one's quick return.
Ever, my daughter, be thou like the dove,—
In friendship as faithful, as constant in love.

What is that, Mother?
                The *Eagle*, my daughter,
Proudly careering his course of joy,
Firm in his own mountain vigor relying,

Breasting the dark storm, the red bolt defying,
His wing on the wind, and his eye on the sun,
He swerves not a hair, but bears onward, right on.
Daughter, may the eagle's flight ever be thine,
Onward and upward, true to the line.

What is that, Mother?
     The *Swan*, my love,
He is floating down from his native grove,
No loved one now, no nestling nigh—
He is floating down by himself to die;
Death darkens his eye, and unplumes his wings,
Yet the sweetest song is the last he sings.
Live so, my love, that when death shall come,
Swan-like and sweet, it may waft thee home.

DIALOGUE.

BY A BOY AND GIRL.

"I WISH I WAS IN THE ARMY."

Mary. Good evening, Charles; I am so glad you have come here this evening.

Charley. Well, Mary, I cannot say that I am glad that I am here.

M. Why, dear Charley, I am sorry to hear you

say that; this is a good place; all the boys and girls are so happy, and our teachers are so glad to see us.

C. That may all be; if they are happy, I am not. I *tell* you, *I did not want* to come.

M. But you astonish me! How strange you talk! You do not want to come here and learn these pretty hymns, and hear our good teachers talk to us about heaven! You do not want to be naughty and wicked, I hope?

C. How foolish you talk, Mary! Do you suppose that every little girl and boy is wicked that don't come to our Sabbath-school?

M. No, Charley, I do not think so; because some may not have shoes to wear, and others may be sick, and cannot come.

C. Yes, and some may go somewhere else.

M. And pray, tell me, Charley, if you wanted to go anywhere else?

C. Yes, I did; and I wish I was there now! I should be happy then; happier than all of you.

M. Why, Charley, what do you mean? You do not wish you was dead, and in heaven?

C. No, but I wish I was——

M. You wish you was where, Charley? Do tell me.

C. I wish—I wish I was in the army. There, you have it now.

M. Where did you get such a foolish idea?—You must have heard Wendell Phillips preach about it.

C. No, I never did. I never heard anybody preach about it.

M. Well, you must have heard some silly man or woman talk about it, or you never would have thought of such a thing. You did not learn it at home.

C. Yes, I did; I learned just such foolish ideas of father and mother, and you need not call them silly, neither.

M. Why, Charley, I know your father and mother. I remember how good and kind they were to me when I called to see your little sister the other day; and I do not believe such a loving father and mother as you have would want their boys to go to the war.

C. You don't think they would, do you? Why, William and Frank, my two big brothers, have been in the army two years; and mother says she wishes she had half-a-dozen more to give to her country.

M. Why, Charley, how strange you talk! Your mother can't love her boys very much, if she wants them to be exposed to all the evils of a camp-life, and risk their lives on the battle-field.

C. Don't love them ! She does love them, and they love her, too ; and they love their country.

M. Well, I heard *my* mother say that none of her family should go to the war. She says they are trying to take away the rights of our Southern brothers, and that it is a *cruel* war, and a " nigger war."

C. All wars are cruel in one sense ; and slavery is, undoubtedly, the cause of this unholy war ; and if, in putting down the rebellion, slavery falls with it, I say, and every true lover of his country will say, amen to it !

M. Well, I cannot see what we have to do with their slaves ; the Constitution gives them the privilege of keeping them, and we have no right to say they shan't, and then go and make war upon them because they would not set them free.

C. We have never said they should not have slaves ; but we have said that they should not establish slavery in territory now free. And we did not make war upon *them.* Don't you remember that they fired the first gun at Fort Sumter, and drove that noble patriot, Major Anderson, and his little faithful band out of it, and took possession of it, and declared that they would not stay in the Union, and would break up this great nation, which had become the home of the free and the asylum of the oppressed of all nations?

M. Why, how eloquent you are! you had better give us a stump speech! But, Charley, now we have been fighting more than three years, and sacrificing a great many of our noblest and best men, and a vast amount of treasure; is it not time to make peace with them and be good friends again?

C. I long for peace as much as you do; but what kind of peace should we have, with those Southern fire-eaters to dictate its terms to us? And the war would have been ended long before this if all had been united at the North.

M. Perhaps it might have been, but I cannot see how. I cannot help *sympathizing* with them

C. That is it; a great many say they feel sorry for them, and say they will not help to put the rebellion down; they oppose enlisting, oppose the draft, and one moment find fault with the Government and the Generals if we lose a battle, and the next rejoice with the rebels over their victories, and then coolly tell us that we might have peace if we wanted it.

M. Well, Charley, after all I cannot see any harm in it.

C. Cannot you see any harm in it? No harm in throwing every obstacle in the way of putting down this wicked rebellion, and thus prolonging the war?

M. Yes; but just think how many have lost their lives, and how many more their limbs!

C. I know all that; but I should rather go to the war and lose my limbs, and my life too, than to remain at home, opposed to the war, and be a despised Copperhead.

M. Copperhead! What are you talking about? What are they, and who are they?

C. They are those who cannot help sympathizing with the rebels, and say that none of their friends shall go to the war; that we are fighting for the nigger, and the Government is all wrong, and they are very clamorous for peace. They are just like the wicked Jews, who tried to heal the trouble among them *slightly,* " saying, peace, when there was no peace."

M. Yes, but are not the Southern people our brothers, and does not the Bible teach us to love our brothers?

C. Brothers? They are not our brothers, they are rebels; they have rebelled against the best government in the world. And what does the Bible say about rebels? When the angels rebelled, did God call them brothers? No! He cast them out of heaven, and no compromise has brought them back. They are traitors to their country, and all those who sympathize with and assist them are partakers with them in an awful sin against God and man; and if they had justice done them they would all be locked up in a dark prison, or hung as high as Haman, to pay the penalty of a violated law. Yes they would—I don't care who they are.

M. Why, you frighten me! I'll go and tell mamma. (*Exit.*)

C. There, that is what I call Southern chivalry; they dare not meet us in open battle, they get behind stone walls, and build masked batteries. Guerrillas—that's what they are. I wish Uncle Abe would call for all the Infant Class boys in the land, and I promise you they would not be trying to get out of the draft, or claiming to be aliens; but every one would shoulder his gun, and, double quick, fall upon them like the locusts of Egypt. I am more anxious to go to the war than ever. I wish I was as big as my teacher, and I wouldn't stay in the city overnight—no, I wouldn't. F.

RECITATION.

BY A BOY OR GIRL.

GOD.

O Thou eternal one! whose presence bright
All space doth occupy—all motions guide;
Unchanged through Time's all-devastating flight—
Thou only God! There is no God beside.
Being above all beings! Mighty One!
Whom none can comprehend and none explore:
Who fill'st existence with thyself alone,
Embracing all—supporting—ruling o'er—
Being whom we call God—and know no more!

In its sublime research Philosophy
May measure out the ocean deep—my count
The sands, or the sun's rays—but God! for Thee
There is no weight or measure; none can mount
Up to thy mysteries. Reason's brightest spark,
Though kindled by thy light, in vain would try
To trace thy counsels, infinite and dark;
And thought is lost ere thought can soar so high,
Even like past moments in eternity.

Thou from primeval nothingness didst call
First chaos, then existence—Lord, on thee
Eternity had its foundation: all
Sprung forth from thee—of light, joy, harmony,
Sole origin—all, all of beauty, Thine.

Thy word created all, and doth create:
Thy splendor fills all space with rays divine.
Thou art, and wert, and shalt be glorious! great!
Life-giving and life-sustaining Potentate!

Thy chains the unmeasured Universe surround;
Upheld by Thee, by Thee inspired with breath!
Thou the beginning with the end hast bound,
And beautifully mingled life and death!
As sparks mount upward from the fiery blaze,
So suns are born, so worlds spring forth from Thee,
And as the spangles in the sunny rays
Shine around the silvery snow, the pageantry
Of Heaven's bright army glitters in thy praise.

A million torches, lighted by thy hand,
Wander unweary through the blue abyss;
They own thy power, accomplish thy command,
All gay with life, all eloquent with bliss.
What shall we call them? Piles of crystal light?
A glorious company of golden streams?
Lamps of celestial ether burning bright?
Suns lighting systems with their joyous beams?
But Thou to these art as the noon to night.

Yes! as a drop of water in the sea,
All this magnificence to thee is lost:—
What are ten thousand worlds compared to Thee?
And what am I, then? Heaven's unnumbered host,
Though multiplied by myriads, and arrayed
In all the glory of sublimest thought,
Is but an atom in the balance weighed
Against thy greatness—is a cypher brought
Against infinity! What am I, then? Naught?

Naught! but the affluency of thy light divine,
Pervading worlds, hath reached my bosom too;
Yes! in my spirit doth thy Spirit shine,
As shines the sun-beam in a drop of dew.
Naught! but I live, and on hope's pinions fly
Eager towards thy presence: for in Thee
I live, and breathe, and dwell; aspiring high,
Even to the throne of thy divinity,
I am, oh God! and surely thou must be!

Thou art! directing, guiding all, Thou art!
Direct my understanding then to Thee;
Control my spirit, guide my wandering heart;
Though but an atom 'midst immensity,
Still I am something, fashioned by thy hand!
I hold a middle rank 'twixt heaven and earth.
On the last verge of mortal being stand,
Close to the realms where angels have their birth,
Just on the boundaries of the spirit land!

The chain of being is complete in me;
In me is matter's last gradation lost,
And the next step is spirit—Deity!
I can command the lightning, and am dust!
A monarch, and a slave! a worm, a God!
Whence came I here, and how? so marvelously
Constructed and conceived? unknown? This clod
Lives surely through some higher energy,
For from itself alone it could not be.

Creator! Yes! Thy wisdom and Thy word
Created me! Thou source of life and good!
Thou Spirit of my spirit, and my Lord!
Thy light, thy love, in their bright plenitude

Filled me with an immortal soul, to spring
Over the abyss of death, and bade it wear
The garments of eternal day, and wing
Its heavenly flight beyond this little sphere,
E'en to its source—to Thee—its author there.

O thought ineffable! O vision blest!
Though worthless our conceptions all of Thee,
Yet shall thy shadowed image fill our breast,
And waft its homage to the Deity.
God! thus above my lonely thoughts can soar;
Thus seek thy presence—Being wise and good;
'Midst thy vast works, admire, obey, adore;
And when the tongue is eloquent no more
The soul shall speak in tears of gratitude.

IN SUNDAY SCHOOL.

Dear Jesus, we've come here to learn of thee,
And we ask for thy Spirit our teacher to be:
Oh, help us to learn, and teach us to pray.
Thou canst see where we stand, and canst hear what we say,

We have not come together for talk, or for play;
Oh no, but to hear what our teacher shall say:
To learn, our dear Saviour, of thee and thy love,
And the home thou hast made for thy children above;

And to learn to be like Thee, as gentle and mild,
So that each of us all may be Thy little child.
Dear Jesus, we ask thee be with us to-day,
And all through the week, at our lessons or play.

RECITATION.

SLANDER.

BY A BOY OR GIRL.

"Slander, that worst of poisons, ever finds
An easy entrance to ignoble minds."

"SLANDER," says Dr. Webster, "is a false tale or report maliciously uttered, and tending to injure the reputation of another by lessening him in the esteem of his fellow-citizens, by exposing him to impeachment and punishment, or by impairing his means of living."

It is a *false report*. Truth, though it may defame and injure, is not slander. Falsehood, if not injurious to our reputation, is not slander. It is a vice—a lie; but it is not slander. A man can be a liar and not a slanderer, but he cannot be a slanderer and not a liar. Slander is the quintessence of many other vices reduced to the most odious compound; an extract of the most poisonous qualities of malice, cowardice, falsehood, and theft.

> "'Tis slander
> Whose edge is sharper than the sword, whose tongue
> Outvenoms all the worms of Nile, whose breath
> Rides on the posting winds, and doth belie
> All corners of the world."

Could you crowd the work of the slanderer into one great warehouse, where at a glance you might see it all; what a scene would you behold! Families in discord—neighbors at variance—innocence sighing over unmerited reproach—friendship of long standing broken—brotherhoods sundered—woes, tears, imprecations—blows and cold-blooded murders. In the midst of all this, the very life and soul of it—the malicious creator of it, moves the slanderer, the hero of the scene, smiling at the ruin he has produced. As Nebuchadnezzar on old Babylon exclaimed, "Is not this great Babylon which I have built?" so he exclaims this great evil is all my own; and he might well add, as he looks upon the scene of wretchedness—

> "I am monarch of all I survey,
> My right there is none to dispute."

The agony of despair, the cruelty of jealousy, the bitterness of revenge, the pining of envy, the groan of outraged innocence, the breaking of hearts—the overwhelming consciousness of injured virtue and reputation—the production of a hell where a heaven might be enjoyed, is glory enough for this most detestable wretch. The thief who robs your house, or picks your pocket, or demands your money with a deadly weapon at your breast, is a gentleman in comparison with the defamer of character. The bard of Avon said it well—

> "Who steals my purse, steals trash: 'twas mine,
> 'Tis his, and has been slave to thousands.
> But he who filches from me my good name,
> Takes that which not enriches him,
> And makes me poor indeed."

Stolen goods may be recovered. Lost money may be found, but when reputation is gone it cannot be regained. The thief who filched from you your good name, may be fined and imprisoned, but he cannot restore what he has stolen.

The slanderer is a reckless invader, marching over the face of society with desolation and death. His great traveling agent, his missionary, sent as a forerunner to prepare the way for his malicious work, is RUMOR; a swift-footed, evil genius, seeming to fly on the winds with evil news. "It is rumored! It is rumored!" Mark how every ear inclined seems to ask, *what?* Putting on the face of astonishment, with a gesture of inquisitive surprise, he asks,—

"Have you heard the news?" No—what? "It is currently reported that Mr. B. told Mr. C. that Mr. D. had heard that Mrs. E. had been informed by Mrs. F. that Mrs. G. had been by some one seen in bad company." Impossible! It cannot be! and yet it may;—sad case! And the crowd of eager listeners, ashamed that they believe such rumor, will repeat it with additions and a glossary to another crowd, and thus rumor flies. What though they are hourly imposed upon, they run to hear the voice of rumor, and listen, and stare, and wonder, and stand aghast, and exclaim "it cannot be," and yet more than half believe it, and tell it over and give it fresh sanctions.

The slanderer is subtle, and puts on a look of wonder. He interludes his speech with many expressions of sorrow and regret. He professes (hypocrite as he is) that he speaks from impulses of friendship, from regard to virtue and truth. He enjoins secrecy. "Don't mention this"—and thus he flies from door to door, making confidents of all; and they in turn repeat it all in confidence, and thus the slander goes.

The most detestable manner of propagating slander is to *surmise*, to intimate by a gesture or a look, that some awful thing is known, but, the backbiter will not tell what. He is more base than the assassin. He plunges the dagger to the heart while he hides behind his dark and lying intimations. But what more can you expect, than a growth in the wickedness of his diabolical profession; what more from a confirmed slanderer than groveling meanness?

Is the picture overdrawn? Are the colorings too deep and dark? Then give the brush to the inspired writers, and let them paint the canvass.— "The words of a tale-bearer are as wounds. When he speaketh fair believe him not, for there are *seven* abominations in his heart." "He is as a mad man who scattereth fire-brands, arrows and death." "My soul is among lions; I lie even among them that are set on fire, even the sons of men, whose teeth are spears and arrows, and their tongue a sharp sword." "The tongue is a fire, a world of iniquity; so is the tongue among our members that defileth the whole body, and setteth on fire the course of nature, and is set on fire of hell." "The tongue can no man tame; it is an unruly evil, full of deadly poison." Nay, then, the picture is not too highly drawn.

Job says the tongue of slander is a "*scourge.*" Its poisonous lashes strike deep into the most sensitive part of our nature. David says it is "*venomous.*" It instils its deadly poison through all the peaceful circles of associated life. Solomon says it is "*destructive.*" It destroys all the fair flowers and shoots which adorn the social scenery. It is the frost of life's summer, a withering, blighting curse. " Its end," says Solomon again, " is *mischievous madness.*" The end of Haman in slandering Mordecai and the Jews was the madness of mischief—the murder of the whole nation. The end of Daniel's accusers was his death. The Jews slandered Jesus Christ in their mischievous madness to procure his death.— Paul in Thessalonica and Berea was charged with treason in mad mischief. Tertullus, the orator and councilor, like too many modern disciples of the same school, because he was "*employed,*" slandered the innocent prisoner, calling him a " pestilent fellow and a mover of sedition." There are devils by profession. But enough. Its evils are more than tongue can utter. " It is evil and only evil, and that continually."

Ye false accusers of bleeding innocence, pause and reflect upon your work. It will not end " in evil and only evil" to your neighbor,—it will return upon your own head. The flame your tongue of fire shall kindle will reach your own dwelling. The "vehement flame" shall consume your social joys, burn into your spirit, and leave you an immortal, living cinder, reprobate, cast out from God, and despised by men. The slanderer raises a tempest which drives his own bark a fearful wreck. He damns his own soul to the deepest hell. He courts and weds eternal burnings. He is a moral plague, a contagious pestilence, a blot on God's fair heritage below; a "deadly wound," whose odious gangrene spreads putrid death over the living face of social happiness. On him will rest in the day of judgment ten thousand slanders, thrown back upon him by the innocent. There he must father his own. Poor wretch! hated, hateful, God-abandoned, lost.

In fine, the slanderer should be feared and shunned. If he stood out before the world, an open enemy, though he were shod with thunder and breathed lightning, and had a volcano in his throat, and poured burning lava from his fire-bosom in a fathomless river of moulten flame across my way, I would not fear him, as in the character of the oil-tongued slanderer who, like a snake in the grass, strikes the poisonous fang deep before you have warning of his attack. I would drive the calumniator of character from my family, as I would a poisonous reptile from my bed.

I would be the friend of all; lay aside the character of a backbiter, and I am his friend; but while he holds that character, I will not, if I know it, stike hands with him. By thus speaking, do I lose friends? I wish to lose them. God forbid that I should be reckoned the friend of the base slanderer. Has he power to injure? If he had a tongue like forked lightning flashing from the depths of the pit, and a throat like a cataract thundering a world of lies forth, I still would not have his friendship. He has no cloak for his sin—no pity in his heart, no truth, no virtue, no moral principle. Some professions are wholly dependent upon reputation for their daily bread. And the slanderer robs their children of even this. -

Were I an artist, and could I sculpture him in all his deformity, or paint him on the canvass, I would clothe him with the gossamer robe of the hypocrite. His eye should smile with a bitter look of subtle malice. His teeth of pointed steel should grin like a horrible picture of death. His tongue should be forked and double like the serpent's. His mouth and throat should emit a livid flame. His breast should be transparent, disclosing corruption, worms and dead men's bones,—an open sepulchre. His heart should beat with the virus of deadly poison

In one hand should be a dagger reeking with blood which drips from its cold blade. The other should have the attitude of defying and menacing the Almighty. One foot should rest upon an orphan slain before him, and the other stand ancle deep in fresh blood. Thunderbolts should be bursting over his head, and lightnings of God's wrath glaring in his face. The dove of peace should be flying from his presence. All round him should be the smouldering ruins he had made. Drear, desolate, and fire-blighted should be the scene, and the ground beneath him should be the crumbling crust of the bottomless pit. In the back ground should be the forms of Jealousy, Despair, Remorse, Hatred and Death. But his character and work could not be transferred to the canvass. It is too odious. No description of it can be hyperbolical. Settle it, then, that the sin of slander is the vilest abomination under the sun, and the slanderer the most dangerous and injurious person which infests and curses the society of mankind.

RECITATION.

THE LITTLE SUNDAY SCHOOL SCHOLAR.

BY A BOY.

I AM a little child indeed,
   And little do I know;
I have not long been taught to read,
   But as I older grow,
I hope I shall the wiser be,
For all the pains bestow'd on me.

I could not tell my letters once,
   Nor read in any book;
Ah! had I still remain'd a dunce,
   How silly should I look,
To say, "This pretty book is mine,"
And yet I could not read a line!

I ought to love the Sunday-school,
   Where with my class I meet,
And all appear—as is the rule—
   So quiet, clean and neat;
And all of us our lessons say,
And learn to read, and sing, and pray.

I ought to love my teachers, too,
   For they are very kind,
To take such trouble as they do,
   To train my youthful mind,

To seek and serve the Lord above,
And know the blessed Saviour's love.

And more than all—much more—I ought
 To praise and love the Lord,
Who caused me early to be taught
 To know his holy Word;
That Word which makes the simple wise,
And tells of joys above the skies.

For though I am a little one,
 I have a soul to save—
A soul for which God's own dear Son
 Himself a ransom gave;
And through his grace the hope is given
That I may dwell with him in heaven.

RECITATION.

THE DISCOURAGED TEACHER.

BY A BOY.

Teacher! lift up thy fainting head;
 O wipe thy tear-filled eye!
Let not thy fervent zeal grow cold,
 Nor let thy courage die;
The promise of thy Saviour stands
 Engraved in fadeless hues;
If thou hast sown in faithfulness,
 The fruit thou shalt not lose.

Thou canst not hope to number here
   The souls which thou hast won,
Nor read the full-writ history
   Of good which thou hast done;
But toil in hope, while life endures,
   And Paradise shall show
Full many a plant thy hand has reared,
   In brightening beauty glow.

Thy tears may flow, but not for fear
   Thy toils should be unpaid;
But, O, let ceaseless torrents fall,
   That souls which God has made,
With eager steps will hurry on
   In sin's deceitful way,
Nor heed the kindly voice and hand
   That seek their course to stay.

Yet, teacher, weary not! still let
   Thy warning accents sound;
Still strive to draw their youthful feet
   From off enchanted ground;
With melting eye and heart, rehearse
   The tale of Jesus' love,
And point to realms of purity,
   And bliss, and joy above.

Thy warning voice and falling tear
   May pass unheeded now—
But, O! dismiss the hopeless grief
   That clouds thy saddened brow!
The seed shall spring, the plant shall bloom,
   And fruit shall yet appear,
And thou in heaven a diadem,
   Thick set with gems, shall wear!

RECITATION.

BY A BOY OR GIRL.

THE BIBLE.

I ADDRESS a Sabbath-school. It will not, therefore, be unappropriate, to speak a few words about that wondrous Book of God which has remained with us till the present time, through all the changes of rising and falling empire—through vicissitude and wo—through gloom and sunshine. Listen, ye lovers of this sacred treasure, while I feebly attempt to shadow forth its immortal beauty and the freshness of its eternal blessings.

Let me draw a picture of a world without a Bible. But how shall I paint a world without a moral Sun? Creation clouds itself in gloom. The stars sink away in their deep and rayless sockets—like the eyes of beauty quenched in death. The feeble taper of human life only burns and throws around it a faint halo of half visible illumination, disclosing only the black and heavy shadows around, like the walls of an impassable sepulchre, where the buried millions of earth await their change, which is only from a dubious animation of an unknown, untried, echoless, annihilation or suspension of being;—nor need they wait long, for sad experience teaches them daily that they stand like soldiers, whose ranks grow thinner and thinner under the blaze and storm of a battle— a battle in which all on both sides are slain, and no one left to howl a lamentation.

Amidst earth's millions no one appears happy.— No one knows of a hereafter with certainty. The nations grope in darkness—thick darkness. But suddenly a ray of light shoots down from heaven, like the first-born light of the virgin creation, and discloses wonders which had been hid for ages. Burning leaves of golden light follow each other in quick succession down from the empyrean. They remain with men, throwing their splendor on all around—while they leave behind them a line of living light which discloses a world to come—an eternity of happiness to the penitent beyond the dark veil of time.

I will now speak of the Grandeur of the Sacred Writings.

Every line from Genesis to the last amen of the apocalypse breathes a spirit not of this world—the grand spirit of its Author. We should be startled to see a magnificent column rising from a desolate plain, rich with splendor, incased with jewels, precious stones and the beauties of an indescribably grand architecture, throwing itself upward through the mist of time until on its capital rested the clear sunlight of immortality. Such a column, amidst the monuments of art and science, is the venerable Bible—the rich, fragrant, perfect, word of God.—Side by side with the grandest poetry, eloquence or literature of the ancient or modern world, the Bible transcends them all in the grandeur of its subject—the beautiful simplicity of its diction, and its unmeasured influence over the minds of men, as well as over their future eternal destinies. The Bible is the only book that shall survive the conflagration of the world. In some form or manner, unscorched by flame, its blessed leaves will be opened on the judgment morning.

In another figure of speech I will call the Bible the Star of Eternity. It has risen over the troubled waters of time. The feeble mariners of earth catch its light over the heaving waves, and, by its pure splendors, they may guide their frail bark into a haven of eternal rest.

I shall call the Bible the Charter of Freedom.—Where, oh ye men of a free republic, would have been *your liberty*, had not Jesus said with an authority, earth and its kings cannot refuse to hear, *Do unto others as ye would have others do unto you?*

Cannot every observer, who regards the signs of the times, notice the increasing influence which the code of inspiration is now exerting on councils, cabinets and kings? Has it not taught, and is it not now teaching in a voice of thunder—that all men are *equal* as well as *free?*

I shall call, in another figure of speech, the Holy Bible the Chart to conduct the soul through the valley of the shadow of death. It is said of the dying Napoleon, that when his features began to sharpen under the approaches of death, he ordered the bust of his far distant infant son to be brought and placed at the foot of his bed. It was an affectionate command. It moves a parent's heart to think of it.— But, oh, could the departing soldier of destiny only have seen the dark future before him made glorious and plain by the light of this Chart of Salvation— could he have caught its holy illustrations flashing heaven and glory upon his darkening eye, he need not have sought earthly alleviations from earthly objects—nor then would the last words of his dying delirium have been the commands of an earthly battle!

In a more affectionate and soothing phrase, I shall call the Bible the comfort of the poor. Softly and gently it lays its hand on the poor man's head—and says—Son, be of good cheer; thy sins may be forgiven thee! Although a few fleeting hours have been spent here below in comparative sorrow and poverty, riches, that never make unto themselves wings to fly away, may be yours, where all sighing and sorrow shall be unknown forever.

The Bible speaks peace to the widow who mourns with unavailing wo the departure of her beloved from her arms and the light of life! It says to her—weep not, for the Almighty is thy husband and protector.

The Bible is the treasure and inheritance of those dear children who have no father and mother to watch over their tender footsteps. The influence which this good gift of heaven is exerting over society in favor of suffering humanity, is even a better security for the welfare of an orphan than an immense legacy of wealth would be.

The Bible is the sailor's friend on the tossing seas. It commands the troubled waves of his soul to be calm, when the horrible deep boils like a pot around and the great monsters of the sea await his going down for their meal. It is like a sheet anchor which he heaves upward, and fastens beyond the clouds, while his bark goes down to the ocean caves, the mermaid haunts and the coral groves.

The Bible is the Christian's monument which we may raise up over the tomb of every dear, departed friend. We look upon its ever-during lines and read of the grand resurrection, when soul and body shall come together again, never to be riven asunder.— We read its storm-defying, golden letters,—Blessed are the dead which die in the Lord : yea, saith the Spirit, from henceforth they shall rest from their labors. J. N. M.

RECITATION.

THE BIBLE.

BY A BOY OR GIRL.

Lamp of our feet! whereby we trace
    Our path, when wont to stray;
Stream from the fount of heavenly grace—
    Brook by the traveler's way.

Bread of our souls! whereon we feed;
    The manna from on high!
Our guide and chart—wherein we read
    Of realms beyond the sky.

Pillar of fire through watches dark!
  Or radiant cloud by day!
When waves would whelm our tossing bark,
  Our anchor and our stay!

Pole-star on life's tempestuous deep!
  Beacon when doubts surround:
Compass by which our course to keep!
  Our deep sea-lead—to sound.

Riches in poverty! our aid
  In every needful hour!
Unshaken rock! the pilgrim's shade,
  The soldier's fortress-tower.

Our shield and buckler in the fight!
  Victory's triumphant palm,
Comfort in grief! in weakness, might!
  In sickness, Gilead's balm.

Childhood's preceptor! manhood's trust!
  Old age's firm ally!
Our hope—when we go down to dust—
  Of immortality!

Pure oracles of truth divine!
  Unlike each fabled dream,
Given forth from Delphi's mystic shrine,
  Or grove of Academe!

Word of the ever-living God!
  Will of His glorious Son!
Without thee how could earth be trod,
  Or Heaven itself be won?

DIALOGUE.

FOR A MAN AND TWO BOYS.

THE BOOT BLACK.

Old Gent. [*reading the paper.*] Well, what is the news? Good, I hope. Ah! here it is (*reads*) "Gen. McClellan removed from the command of the army of the Potomac—Gen. Burnside takes his place. The army in tears—and in motion!" Well, well, well! Our country is ruined! We may as well give up the contest! McClellan superseded! The President is surely beside himself! But that is not all—the army is in *motion*, and on the road to Richmond—to ruin! But stocks are up. Ah! ha! that's encouraging—that's good! Ah! ha! and here's the cause: (*reads*) "A glorious Victory! 100,000 of the enemy killed—A perfect rout and utter defeat—No loss on our side—Particulars in second edition."

[*Enter Boot Black.*] Black your boots, sir? black your boots? Do it cheap. Only five cents! Make 'em shine like a dollar. (*aside*) Wonder can the old gentleman hear? (*Begins brushing the boots, singing* "John Brown's body.")

Old Gent. Oh, here it is—Evening Express, second edition. "Further particulars of the great fight—Confirmation of the Victory! A single regiment of housemaids, while marching through their respective kitchens, were attacked by over 100,000 cockroaches! but each of them, being well armed with a bottle of Lyon's Magnetic Powder, charged upon the enemy, who skedaddled with great precipitancy, leaving 100,000 dead and wounded on the field of battle! The only loss sustained by us was a few loads of provisions carried away in their retreat by the half-starved foe." (*Indignant.*) Stuff and nonsense! Lyon's Powder indeed! Hang the fellow! There ought to be a den of such Lions, and he among them. Fort Lafayette is too good for him.

[Enter Boot Black, singing "John Brown's body," also Newsboy, who pins label, "Death to Cockroaches—Lyon's Powder," on old gent's. coat, saying "look here," and leaves, crying "Herald—Times—Tribune."]

Old Gent. (rising to his feet.) Hi, ho, hello! what's all this noise about? Five Points let loose! Out of this place, you bad boys! Mr. Sexton, put these boys off the stage—put them off, sir! We might as well try to hold our Anniversary in the open street! Dear me! the country's ruined! [Boot Black retreats, but immediately returns.]

Boot Black. Please, sir, let me finish that job—got one boot nearly done. Do it for half price. I'm very poor.

Gent. Can't do it, my poor boy. Don't you see this

large audience waiting for the stage? They are expecting a number of performers here immediately.

Newsboy. I know it, sir—but they've all got good homes to go to when it's over, and I've not a place in all the world to sleep till I have earned the price of a night's lodging.

Gent. Well, well—when the performances are over, I'll see you in the lower hall, and arrange it. Come now, be quick!

Boot Black. Please, sir, mayn't I stay and see them? I'd like to see them, sir; and it's so cold below in the hall—won't charge nothin' for the boots if you'll let me.

Gent. But you're too dirty, my poor boy, and too ragged!

Boot Black. I'll clean myself in a minute, sir. It will only take me a minute. [Takes from his pocket a very dirty handkerchief, wipes his face, making it blacker than before.] Now, I'm all right!

Gent. "All right," indeed! why, you look more like a blacked boot than like a Boot Black. Another such wipe and a few passes of your brush, and your face will shine like a shoe. Oh, no, that'll never do! Go to the Sexton, and get some water and a towel and wash yourself properly.

Boot Black. Please, sir, I never uses water in that way. They say it spiles the skin, sir. I always *rubs* it off.

Gent. Well, I hope you generally succeed better than now; but as you appear very anxious to stay, I'll ask these kind-hearted children for their consent.—

(*Addresses the audience.*) Dear children, this poor boy has found his way to the stage, and asks your permission to remain to witness the performances. Shall he be allowed the privilege?

A Voice. Yes, if he will sing us a song.

Another Voice. And makes a speech.

Gent. You have heard the decision. What will you do?

Boot Black. Do my best, sir, if you will help me.

Gent. Well, let us have a song first. What do you know?

Boot Black. I knows "John Brown's body," "My Johnny was a Shoemaker," "The Soap-fat Man," and "The Gallant 69th."

Gent. Perhaps the children will assist you in singing "Marching along." (*The scholars sing.*) Now for the speech.

Boot Black. What shall I say, sir?

Gent. Well, tell them who you are, and what you are, and when and where you was born, and what you do for a living, and all about it.

Boot Black. Very well, sir—I'll try. (*Addresses the School.*) SPEECH.—I am a poor, wandering, houseless, homeless boot black: but I'm not a beggar. My father is dead. Mother is in heaven. Bridget is married to Rory the rag-man, and brother Phil has gone to the war to be kilt. My name is Barney, and I'm proud of it, for it's the name my mother gave me. A name and a blessing was all she had to give. I was too young to remember when I was born, but Charley, that keeps the candy stand on Centre-street, will tell you all about it if you'll ax him. I'm a City Park boot black, and I'm not ashamed of my profession.— With a box of Day & Martin's best blacking, these old brushes of mine, and a fine day, I can see my face in a gentleman's boot as soon as any boy in the Park. It was good of ye's to let me stay here to-night, ladies and gentlemen; and it's in my heart to bless ye's for it. Och! and don't I wish I had the feet of ye's all in two great boots here on this stand of mine, and wouldn't I put the shine on them, my honies! Oh, no, of course not! A boot black has no heart, of course not! He's not thankful to nobody nor nother! Is it so, kind friends? Oh, no. He has a heart—a heart that feels and bleeds too sometimes. If you're kind to him, he'll never forget you—if you'll love him, he'll love the very boots you stand in. My mother loved me once, but she's in heaven now. One cold, cold day, as long ago as I can remember, she called me to her bed-side on the floor, and said she to me: "Oh, Barney, I'm going to lave you dear—be a good boy, and meet me in heaven, darlint!" "Mother dear," said I, "where is it—where is heaven?" She pointed to the ceiling and whispered, "Up there, Barney darlint, up there—meet me up there." My heart was broke entirely, and it is breaking again to-night at the thoughts of her. Kind friends! I want to meet my mother in heaven. Will you show me the way? I am wicked, ragged, and dirty; but my mother loves me still, and I know she's waiting for me up there in heaven."

Gent. What shall we do, children? Shall we take some of our missionary money to clothe this poor boy, and admit him to our Sunday-school, and show him the way to Jesus, to heaven, and to his mother? (Voice, Yes, yes.) Let us sing for him "The Beautiful Land" where his mother has gone. (School sing.)

CHRISTMAS ADDRESS,

FOR ONE OF "OUR LAMBS."

Perhaps you'd like to know, kind friends,
    What brings an infant here
On a public stage, at this tender age,
    Inviting your listening ear.

Be very quiet then, kind friends,
    Or my voice you cannot hear—
And I'll tell you as well as a child can tell
    The reason I now appear.

I'm a lamb of the flock, kind friends,
    The little flock you love,—
The fold where we meet is under your feet,
    There's another fold above.

The Saviour's our Shepherd, kind friends,
    A tender Shepherd too,—
In beautiful lays we sing his praise
    As birds of the forest do.

And this is Christmas-day, kind friends,
    The day of our Shepherd's birth,—
From heaven he came, in his Father's name,
    To visit his flock on earth.

And He was once a lamb, kind friends,
    A little lamb like me;
But they pierced his side, and our Shepherd died,
    And a dying Lamb was He.

He lives in heaven now, kind friends,
    And, from his Father's throne,
He bids us arise, and haste to the skies,
    For He claims us for His own.

And are you all His sheep, kind friends?
    Feeding on pastures green?
Do your hearts rejoice when you hear His voice,
    Though the Shepherd be unseen?

And now adieu, adieu, kind friends!
    My simple tale I've told,—
I've told you as well as a lamb can tell
    Of the Saviour's little fold.

RECITATION.

JARIUS' DAUGHTER.

BY A BOY OR GIRL.

See that weeping father! In heartfelt anguish he is watching his darling child, who is fast sinking into the cold, dreary grave. Hear him cry, as he sees the death-damp gather on her marble brow, "My child! my child! art thou passing from my sight forever? Couldst thou not have lingered here a little longer, to cheer the declining years of thy poor lonely father? For twelve years thou hast been the delight of my heart. But now thy lovely eyes are closed forever! Thy sweet voice will no more be heard ringing through the now desolate dwelling. Thou art dying! Death has touched my flower, and she has faded. Oh, my child! how can I give thee up! Can nothing save her? Is there no balm in Gilead? No physician there that can cure my darling? No, all, all has failed. My child—my only child must die! But, stop! methinks I've heard of One, the Prophet of Gallilee, who not long since wiped the tears from the eyes of the widow of Nain. Her only son was dead; the man whom they call Jesus chanced to pass by that way.

His heart was touched with compassion when he saw the lonely mother weep. He bade her dry her tears. He spoke to the young man, and he lived again. I have heard that He refuses none that come to Him—how He heals the broken-hearted. Perhaps He will pity me, and give me back my treasure. I'll go to Jesus. I'll tell Him I love my child. I'll ask Him just to speak that word, and she'll live." He went to Jesus. He fell at his feet. He poured into the Saviour's sympathizing ear his tale of sorrow. He besought Him to come, and touch his child that she might recover. The Saviour listened to his prayer. He goes with him to the chamber where lay the cherished one. He sees the little form lying cold and still. Death has performed his work—he has pierced with his invincible dart that little, loving heart, and it has ceased to beat. He sees the tears of the stricken parents. He knows how they mourn for their lost darling, and gently saying unto them "Be not afraid, believe only," He who is the resurrection and the life takes the emaciated hand within His own, and speaks the life-giving word, and behold! the little maid arose! Intelligence again beamed from her bright eyes. Her little arms, no longer bound by the grim monster, are ready to embrace her delighted but astonished parents,—her tongue to praise Him who has raised her from the power of death and the grave. She is alive again! What joy now reigns where but a few moments before sorrow had spread her sable wings! What love the happy parents bore to that Saviour who had done so much for them!

My dear little schoolmates! it was that same Saviour who so dearly loves little children, and who when He was on earth took them in His arms and blessed them, and said: "Suffer little children and forbid them not to come unto me, for of such is the kingdom of heaven." Do we love that Saviour who loves us so well? Do we remember that He is grieved every time we speak a naughty word or do anything wrong? He died for us, and was laid in the cold, dark tomb: but He is in heaven now, where He watches all we say and do. But one day He will appear again, and all His holy angels with Him, and all the dead shall hear His voice and come out of their graves. Then all the good shall have bright crowns of glory given unto them, and they shall reign with the Saviour forever. But all the wicked shall be punished. Let us, my dear schoolmates and friends, try to live so that we shall be among the happy number to whom it shall be said: "Come, ye blessed of my Father, inherit the kingdom prepared for you from the foundation of the world."

RECITATION.

BY A BOY.

"IN FOGY TIMES."

In fogy times, when men were slow,
And women very good, you know—
When boys would hardly dare to grow,
Unless their daddies told them so—
When mothers staid at home to spin
The wool, to dress their "darters" in,
And would have deemed it mortal sin
Had Sally wished a " bussum" pin—
When maidens dared their years to tell,
   E'en though above the teens they rose;
When hoops graced not the village belle,
   To captivate her rustic beaux,--
Then pedagogues were very few,
   And pretty school marms scarcer still,
Went boarding round, the season through,
   Till " sass" and dough-nuts paid their bill.
Then Johnny learned his A, B, C,
   Most happy if his name he writ;
And if he reached the " Rule of Three,"
   For any station he was fit.

Then, sons in time to manhood grew,
    True scions of the parent stock,
Prepared to wend life's journey through,
    Endure the strife, withstand each shock.
Then men were "Democrats" at birth,
    And nursed the creed thro' tender years:
Then horrid isms had no worth,
    And CUFFE had not roused their fears:
Then churches had no pews to let,
    Nor steeples towering in the air—
Nor preachers who, their pay to get,
    Would careful be great sins to spare.
But humble was the house of prayer,
The awful fiddle was not there;
To guard against the wicked heart,
The girls and boys were kept apart.
Thus jogged our country slowly on,
    Till fairly woke, by press and steam,
It sprung to action, and anon
    We swiftly glide, on Progress' stream,
To glory—honor—and renown,—
And stand to-day with awful frown
On rebel subjects, traitors grown.
Should bluster "Bull" or arch "Capen"
    Invade our soil, to help the wrong,
We'll call on GOD, and strike a blow
    For Freedom! and it won't be long
Before our Flag of golden stars
Shall triumph o'er the Southern "bars"—
And all the world, with loud acclaim,
Will honor and respect our name!   G. W. D.

DIALOGUE.

DAVID AND JONATHAN.

(CHARACTERS—JONATHAN, DAVID, MERAL, MICHAL & SAUL).

Scene I. David and Jonathan. Jonathan dressed as prince.

Jonathan. My best friend David! you have delivered the nation—you have saved the throne of my father. What can I do for you as a testimony of my regard?

David. My dearly beloved Jonathan, I claim no honor to myself in this matter. Jehovah has been my strength: he directeth the weapons of death, and delivered the mighty Goliath into my hand. To God be all the praise.

J. But God has honored you as the instrument of our deliverance. The armies of Israel were defied and were terror-stricken; but now the mighty foe is vanquished, and I look upon you as our deliverer. You are much more entitled to be the Prince than I am. I mean to transfer all my honors to your noble self.

D. O Jonathan! my beloved Jonathan! your friendship surpasses all bounds. I see that our hearts are knit together as one; and I feel assured that they shall never be severed, save by death: but dismiss these thoughts now, my dear brother.

J. I cannot dismiss them. I must give vent to the overpowering feelings of my heart. God is working for you, and I know that he will fix you on the throne of Israel. Here, take my robe [puts it on D.,] and here is my girdle [hands it to D.,] and my sword also [D. fastens the girdle on him and receives the sword. Immediately a company *unseen* sing] "Daughter of Zion, awake from thy sadness," &c. [and between each verse a company of Infant-class scholars respond]— "Saul hath slain his thousands and David his ten of thousands."

[Enter two daughters of Saul, MERAL and MICHAL.]

Meral. What means all this excitement? (to Jonathan.) Is my brother so base as to seek to overthrow my father's throne? I heard your conversation, and shall tell my father at once.

Michal. (To David.) Why, David, I did not think you had designs against my father's kingdom!

D. I disclaim all such designs. You misunderstand our interview. How can I help what the people sing? If God inspires them, who shall complain?

Michal. Of course, you will not complain when the import is to place you on the throne. But my father was chosen of God and anointed by Samuel, and has *alone* the legal right.

D. I tell you plainly, I seek not the throne. I am unworthy. I am incapable of filling it with honor.—

No such thought as you impute to me ever entered my mind.

J. My sisters, begone ! you have nothing to do with the matter anyway. It is my inheritance, and I understand my own business. Depart at once [they go.]

D. And now I know that they will tell the king, and my life will be in jeopardy.

J. No, it shall not. I will die for you any time rather than *you* should be sacrificed. I will dissuade my father. I know he thinks a great deal of you : he knows you have redeemed the nation.

D. But, my dear Jonathan, I have, somehow, a sad foreboding that evil awaits me. But let us go to the king, and explain all. (Exit.)

SCENE SECOND.—[Royal palace—King Saul on his throne—two daughters on his right ; on the left officers and attendants. Enter David & Jonathan : they approach the king and bow before him.]

David. My lord the king——

Saul. Be still. I know it all. You are conspiring against my throne. They ascribe to me thousands and to you tens of thousands ; but I will let you know that I am able to maintain my authority and my kingdom.

J. My father ! oh king——

Saul. I will have none of your insolence : out of my presence. The very next tidings of this nature, and your lives shall pay the forfeit. (Exit D. and J.)

Saul. [Soliloquy.] But, let me see. It will not do to wait. They no doubt will proceed in their nefarious plans, and a little delay may cost me my life, and my throne. I will pursue them at once, and we will see what will become of his "tens of thousands." (To Captain-General) You will at once prepare me three thousand choice men, and I will pursue David forthwith. (Exit king and court.)

    Scene Third.—[The king has been pursuing David unsuccessfully, and lies down in a cave and falls asleep. David enters alone, walks softly to the king, takes his sword and cuts off a piece of the king's robe and takes his spear. King awakes and rises.]

Saul. What means all this?

David. My lord the king (holds up the robe's piece and spear) be it known that I do not stretch forth my hand against the Lord's anointed. My father, see! yea, see the skirt of thy robe—thy life was in my hand, yet I killed thee not. Now see that no evil is in my heart against thee. The Lord judge between me and thee this day.

Saul. Is this thy voice, my son David? Thou art more righteous than I. Thou hast rewarded me good for evil; and now I know that thou shalt surely be king, and the nation shall be established in thy hand.

David. My father, take thy spear. (Exit.)

    Scene Fourth.—David and Jonathan meet.

J. Well, the Lord be praised! We still live to enjoy each other's society.

D. Yes, my dear brother, the Lord is with us; and although thy father sought thy life, God frustrated his design, and gave me a decided advantage over him— but I spared him, and I hope he will love me now.

J. No, no, my dear friend. I know his heart—he is all envy. He will still seek to take revenge on you; only get in his power once, and your life is gone.

D. O, Jonathan! it cannot be,—you must be mistaken. He said to me: "Is this thy voice, my son David?" and his voice was in the tone of kindness.— Indeed he must see now that I would do him no harm.

J. Well, my beloved David, my bosom friend! I will watch events, and inform you. But I must go now —duty calls me. The Philistines are upon us, and threaten our destruction. I must go with my father to defend the nation. Good by for now. I will be with you soon. (Exit.)

Scene Fifth.—[David is musing alone, when a messenger arrives with sad tidings.]

D. From whence comest thou?

Messenger. Out of the camp of Israel am I escaped.

D. How went the matter? I pray thee tell me.

Mess. The people are fled, many are fallen and dead, and Saul and Jonathan are dead also.

D. (mourns exceedingly.) O, the beauty of Israel is fallen upon the high places! How are the mighty fallen! Tell it not in Gath; publish it not in the streets of Askelon, lest the daughter of Philistia rejoice —lest the daughter of the uncircumcised triumph. O,

Jonathan! thou wast slain in thy high places. How are the mighty fallen in the midst of the battle! I am distressed for thee, my brother Jonathan! Very pleasant hast thou been unto me. Thy love was passing the love of woman. How are the mighty fallen, and the weapons of war perished! (Enter Meral & Michal.)

Meral. O, what shall we do now that the nation be saved? It will not do to mourn and weep when danger is at our doors. Is there no one to deliver Israel?

Michal. O yes, David will lead our armies to victory. Our father is dead, and Jonathan is slain also. Truly now David will take the throne and deliver Israel.

Meral. It belongs to our brother, Meple Basheth; and if not to him, then to me. I will succeed my father. I will be queen.

Michal. My sister, you talk foolishly. Do you not know that David was anointed by the prophet Samuel when very young? how the prophet went to the house of old Jesse, and by direction of God had all his twelve sons pass before him, and the Lord chose David? and Samuel then took out his horn of oil and anointed him, in God's name, future king of Israel.

Meral. Is it so, my sister? Then I submit. The Lord forgive my selfishness. David shall have the throne, and rule us. Here, David, take the crown—(takes it and places it on David's head,) God bless king David!

David. My soul is too full for utterances to-day.— My dearest friend on earth is gone, and even royal glories cannot comfort me; and furthermore, we have no time for words. I must gird on my sword, and try and deliver Israel. I must quit the throne for a season, until the Lord of battles shall give me victory over Israel's foes, and enable me to establish the nation in righteousness : and to Jehovah be all the glory!

J. H. V.

RECITATION.

THE KISS IN SCHOOL.

BY A BOY.

A DISTRICT school not far away,
'Mid Berkshire's hills, one winter's day,
Was humming with its wonted noise
Of threescore mingled girls and boys—
Some few upon their tasks intent,
But more on future mischief bent;
The while the master's downward look
Was fastened on a copy-book—
Rose sharp and clear a rousing smack!
As 'twere a battery of bliss
Let off in one tremendous kiss.
"What's that?" the startled master cries,
"That, thir," a little imp replies,

"Wath Willion Willith, if you please—
I thaw him kith Thuthannah Peathe!"
With frown to make a statue thrill,
The master thundered, "Hither, Will!"
Like wretch o'ertaken in his track,
With stolen chattels on his back,
Will hung his head with fear and shame,
And to that awful presence came,
A great, green, bashful simpleton,
The butt of all good-natured fun.
With smile suppressed and birch upraised,
The threat'ner faltered, "I'm amazed
That you, my biggest pupil, should
Be guilty of an act so rude!
Before the whole set school, to boot—
What evil genius put you to't?"
"'Twas she herself, Sir," sobbed the lad,
"I did'nt mean to be so bad—
But when Susannah shook her curls,
And whispered I was 'fraid of girls,
And darsn't kiss a baby's doll,
I couldn't stand it, Sir, at all!
But up and kissed her on the spot;
I know—boo-hoo—I ought to not,
But somehow from her looks—boo-hoo—
I thought she kind o' wished me to."

W. P. P.

COLLOQUY.

MY BIBLE.

FOR ONE BOY AND FOUR GIRLS.

(*Boy enters with a small Bible open in his hand.*)

Boy. Oh, book divine! A precious treasure! My mother's gift! her last bequest. I would not sell thee for all the gold of earth! nor diamonds fair, nor all the jewelled treasures of the earth combined. Thou art my joy and comfort, the solace of my lonely hours. Thou dost remind me of my mother dear. Could men bestow on me all wealth and fame, and all the pleasures of the world for thee, my Bible! they could not have thee. (*Sits down.*) [Enter]

Infidelity. Well, my boy, thou seem'st most deeply engaged. Thou must have some interesting book.

Boy. Interesting, did you say? Oh, how interesting! This is the Bible my mother gave me when she died. I should think every one would like to read it. Don't you, sir?

Infidelity. Well, I read it sometimes, but I don't know that it is so interesting. But, my boy, had thy mother no better gift for thee?

Boy. No better gift ! why, sir, you talk strange.—I thought this was the best of all gifts. My mother told me so.

Infidelity. But why do you prize it so much higher than other books? What good can it do, or what can you do with it?

Boy. I prize it because it is the word of God, and it tells us about the Saviour, who loved us and died for us. And it tells of heaven, the place where all the good are gathered. It teaches me the way to live. This is its value, and this the good it accomplishes.

Infidelity. But, you don't believe there is a God, do you? and a heaven, such as that you speak of?

Boy. Believe it, sir? Why, what should I believe if I did not? I do believe it. But you, sir, talk like a man who came to our house before mother died, and she said he was an infidel, because he did not believe the Bible. Are you an infidel, sir?

Infidelity. I suppose I am, if disbelieving that book makes me one.

Boy. Well, ain't you sorry you are an infidel, sir?

Infidelity. Why, boy, what should I be sorry for?

Boy. Because my mother used to say, the men who talked as you do, made themselves out no better than the brute creation; and I would be sorry if I thought myself no better than they. I think this book speaks of those who reason as you do.

Infidelity. Poor, deluded boy! all the bright prospects of his future years are blighted and that forever. (Exit.)

Boy. Why, he has left me! He don't like to hear the Bible read I guess. (Sings, "The Bible, the Bible, more precious than gold.") [Enter]

Wealth. Welcome, boy! strange music I heard just now. I was attracted by its melody, but surprised at its sentiment.

Boy. How so, lady?

Wealth. Didst thou not say, "The Bible, the Bible, more precious than gold"?

Boy. I did—and is it not so, lady?

Wealth. Why, boy, who taught thee so? Strange parents thou must have had! "The Bible more precious than gold"! Why, boy, thou knowest not what thou sayest. Think a moment. That Bible is a poor dependence. It will make you miserable beyond description. Cast it away, and come with me, and we will work together and get houses and lands and wealth in abundance, and all the pleasures of the world shall be ours.

Boy. (Reads from the Bible.) "Lay not up for yourselves treasures upon earth, where moth and rust doth corrupt; but lay up for yourselves treasures in heaven."

Wealth. And dost thou think that treasures in heaven are of more consideration than the treasures of earth? And that some future hope is better than present enjoyment? Oh! cast away such thoughts, and let us get wealth and enjoy our life while we may.

Boy. (Reads.) "Riches take to themselves wings, and flee away; and if riches increase, set not your heart upon them." These, my lady, are worthy of consideration.

Wealth. My boy, look yonder. Those beautiful houses, those walks and gardens, those lovely flowers, ever blooming and ever beautiful ; those fields of enamelled splendor ; those forest groves that line yon mountain side ; that crystal stream that sings its way along and slakes the thirst of merry birds whose chanting tunes are sweetest melody. All these are mine. It was gold that purchased them ; your Bible would not.

Boy. But it says, "What profit hath a man if he gain the whole world and lose his own soul?" And then we have this encouragement : "Seek first the kingdom of God and his righteousness, and all these things shall be added unto you." Job, you know, had them all given him.

Wealth. But, my boy, canst thou not seek with me for wealth, and still retain thy Bible ? Thou art young and in blooming health ; long life is before thee. Thou canst enjoy much of the pleasures of wealth ; and in future years thou canst lay up treasures in heaven.

Boy. Yes, lady, but my Bible tells me, "it is easier for a camel to go through the eye of a needle than for a rich man to enter the kingdom of God"—and then, lady, should I consent to go with you, and accumulate all the pleasures you have mentioned, do you not remember that Solomon tried them all even to greater extent than yourself, and he called them "all vanity"? Should I try an experience with a prospect of so little satisfaction ?

Wealth. (Turning away) Silly youth! he thinks his Bible of more value than gold, or silver, or the pleasures that lie in such rich profusion around us. (Exit.)

Boy. (Sings) "The Bible, the Bible, blest volume of truth," &c. [Enter]

Pleasure. Pleasant youth, thou art fair and lovely. Many years are before thee. Thou dreamest no doubt of much pleasure. I see thine eye is sparkling, and beams with youthful delight. Thy step is elastic and sprightly as the fawn's. The spring-time is blooming all around thee, and the cup of pleasure is before thee. Oh, taste it, my boy, it is yours.

Boy. Why, lady, thou seemest like some sweet messenger! thou talkest well! pray tell me thy name.

Pleasure. Pleasure, my boy; I hope to be thy companion.

Boy. Pleasure thy name? Where goest thou, and what is thy occupation?

Pleasure. I go to the remotest parts of earth. I traverse the continents and the oceans, the mountains and the plains. I am found on the rapid steamers of the west and the more gentle gondolas of the east. In the cities and in the villages I am found in the congregations of men, and I cheer the hearts of desponding humanity. I cause music to flow in unceasing harmony, and they who enjoy my company are filled with continual delight. Am I not to be desired? Seek for me, boy, and thou shalt be my companion.

Boy. Ah! well hast thou spoken. Thou well nigh

persuadest me. Thou art fair and enticing, but I cannot be thy companion.

Pleasure. And why canst thou not? What other companion wouldst thou seek?

Boy. See here, lady, this (holding out his Bible) is my counsellor—let me read : "He that loveth wine and oil shall not be rich, and he that loveth pleasure shall be a poor man."

Pleasure. Ah ! my boy, wilt thou be deceived by that book ? Thou art young—life with thee may be scenes of continued pleasure. 'Twill do for the gray-headed to talk thus. Come with me, and let us enjoy pleasure while we may. I read from that book, "eat, drink, and be merry."

Boy. Hear me, lady : (reads) "She that liveth in pleasure is dead while she liveth."

Pleasure. And wilt thou still be deceived ? Thou talkest very unwisely. Wilt thou deprive thyself of all pleasure ? Art thou willing to forego all the amusements that surround thee ? live a life of seclusion, and die unhonored and unknown ?

Boy. Yes, lady, all this if need be. Hear me :— (reads) "Remember now thy Creator in the days of thy youth : when the evil days come not, and the years draw nigh when thou shalt say I have no pleasure in them."

Pleasure. Ah ! my boy, thou art preparing thyself for a miserable existence. See that hall of festive mirth, where the youth and beauty of the land are gathered. Hark! do you not hear that music as it floats upon the evening air? and those voices, tokens of merry hearts within? Hast thou no desire to mingle there and join with them where pleasure reigns supreme?

Boy. No, lady, no. Thy words are pleasant to the ear, but hear me: (reads) "I made me garlands and orchards, and I planted trees in them of all kinds of fruits: I got me men-singers and women-singers, and the delights of the sons of men, as musical instruments and that of all sorts. Then I looked on the works that my hands had wrought, and all was vanity."—Oh, lady, entice me not again.

[Enter WEALTH and FAME.]

Pleasure. Good evening, sisters! 'tis well thou art come.

Fame. How so?

Pleasure. You see yonder youth, intent upon his book? A bright, but most infatuated boy—one who would make our company complete. He's pleasant, yet at times I think him sad. He's poring now among the rusty pages of his mother's Bible. No worldly pleasure will arrest him.

Wealth. I know him well. I labored with him long that he might have all wealth and that abundantly, and still he wished it not; and yet he seems an honest lad.

Pleasure. (To Fame) Perhaps, my sister, thou canst win him to our company.

Wealth. (To Fame) Try, my sister.

Fame. We'll approach the lad. I am glad to meet thee, my lad ; that book must be a pleasant companion.

Boy. Yes, lady, the only one I have.

Fame And do you wish no other ?

Boy. I never yet have wished for any other. I find it very pleasant company. This book is all that's left me now. Once it was my mother's, and when she died she placed it in my hand, and said, "My son, this is the way of life. It taught *me* how to live. Study it, my son, and bind its precepts on thy heart." Already I have become deeply interested in it.

Fame. Truly, a book of much value. But, my boy, it should not be your constant study. The world has other charms for thee ; and good as you may think your book, 'twill not advance you among the sons of men. Your book should only be the counsel for the aged and infirm. 'Tis good for them to know its truth; but you, my lad, should fill your mind with thoughts of a different nature.

Boy. Wouldst thou deceive me, lady ? Thy words seem very strange !

Fame. Deceive thee, boy ! most surely I would not. But listen—I have a message for thee. My mission in the world is one of high renown. No one in life succeeds without my help. I have the power to bestow all praise and honor on the sons of men. The brightest names recorded on the scroll of fame was only through my assistance. Those that court my pleasure are sure of success. Come ! come with me, and thy name shall not be unknown. Thou shalt be the companion of the great ones of earth, and thy influence shall be wide and extended.

Boy. But, lady, how can I attain all this? I read in my Bible: "Acknowledge him in all thy ways, and He will direct thy paths."

Fame. Yes, and your book encourages you to be my companion, for it says: "Rejoice, oh young man, in thy youth; and let thy heart cheer thee in the days of thy youth, and walk in the ways of thine heart and in the sight of thine eyes." So, come, and be my companion without further hesitancy.

Boy. But, lady, I read that "for all these things God will bring thee into judgment."

Fame. And dost thou believe it? Think a moment. Wilt thou be content to live alone in the world, a life of ignorance, and among those from whom it is an honor to be secluded?

Boy. Ah, lady! I fear to tread the paths that thou wouldst lead me. I know but little of the world—its pleasures, its honors, or its fame. But this I must remember, ever to cherish the dying counsel of my mother. She told me this book should be my chart of life! and when she died she embraced me in her arms, while tears were flowing down her cheeks, and said— "My son, when I am carried to the silent grave, and you are left alone, then learn the truths this book contains, and thou wilt have all wealth and pleasure and honor, such as worldly fame can never bestow." These were my mother's dying words.

Fame. I would not counsel thee, my boy, to violate

thy mother's last request; but if thou'lt be my companion, the glory of the world, and high renown, and all that's great among the sons of men, shalt be thine own. Thy presence shall be sought for and thy influence equal to thy desire.

Boy. No, lady, no. I cannot, for I read—"The fear of the Lord is the beginning of wisdom," and that "the righteous shall be recompensed in the earth."— This is all my desire.

Fame. I had hoped to have had thy company: perhaps some future time thou wilt think more favorably of my offer. Farewell. (Retires to her companions.)

Boy. Farewell! (Reads) "Happy is the man that findeth wisdom, and the man that getteth understanding, for the merchandize of it is better than the merchandize of silver, and the gain thereof than fine gold. She is more precious than rubies, and all the things that thou canst desire are not to be compared to her. Length of days are in her right hand, and in her left hand riches and honor. Her ways are ways of pleasantness, and all her paths are paths of peace."

[Enter] *Wisdom.* Didst I not hear thee enquiring for me, my boy?

Boy. And what is thy name, lady?

Wisdom. I am Wisdom, whom thou seekest. What wouldst thou, my boy?

Boy. O, I would learn of thee the truths this book contains. I am but a poor and friendless boy. 'Tis but a short time since my mother died. The world since then has had but little charm: though Pleasure,

Wealth, and Fame surround me, yet I find but little interest in them all. This (holding out his Bible) was my mother's last bequest. Its pages I have read, and learned that Wisdom is the greatest treasure we can possess. Is it not so, lady?

Wisdom. Yes, my good boy—in taking Wisdom for thy guide, thou hast a treasure greater than all beside. That book is a good counsellor. Thy mother could not have bestowed on thee a better nor a richer gift. Value it above all wealth, or pleasure, or fame.— Through all the toilsome years of life, let it be thy guide; and when thou art old, still will it cheer thee and be thy solace and comfort.

Boy. Thou shalt be my guide and counsellor.

All. And we will seek her too.

Scholars sing—" We'll not give up the Bible."

R. A.

RECITATION.

BY A BOY.

THE LOST CHILD.

The night comes in, and the storm is wild,
    There's a biting blast and a driving sleet,
    And up and down each lonely street
The criers call, "Lost child! lost child!"

What, a little one this bitter night
    ALONE and LOST in this howling storm?
Oh God! be merciful, we pray,
    And shield the tender form.

Speed, speed thee, rider! scream the cry;
    He may be frozen and crushed and dead!
A mother waits for her laughing boy—
    And canst thou take her a corpse instead?

Speed, speed thee, rider! and mark the print
    Of little feet across the snow,
And call the fathers from every house
    Upon your search to go.

And while ye seek, let a louder voice,
    One that the whole wide world can hear,
Break out above the howling storm
    In tones most thrilling, loud, and clear—

Lost, in the stormy night of sin,
    An orphan, the child of his mother's vow :
'Tis years and years since he wandered away;
    Christians, turn out and seek for him now.

Lost, from a mother one sunny day,
    A little girl with a blue dove eye;
She hath lost her way to heaven, and now
    She hath fallen in woe to die.

Lost, from the pasture, many a lamb
    That wander'd away when shepherds did sleep;
And now they are roving, God only knows where,
    HE ONLY can hear their shivering bleat.

Lost, lost! and the night drifts in—
    Children more than you'll ever find—
Turn out! turn out! and with pity seek
    And bring them in from the storm and the wind.

Perchance your little ones are gone,
    And their feet will never turn back again.
Haste, father! haste, and follow their track,
    Mark every spot where they have been :

And if ye find them, thank your God,
    For many a mother is wailing to-night
For a birdling lost that she'll never find,
    Not even in heaven's morning light.

RECITATION.

THE MILITIA CAPTAIN.

BY A BOY.

Friends, Citizens, Fellow-countrymen, and Soldiers: This is a tearin' country, and has got an amazin' good start among the white nations of the earth. Does any one ask, "What makes it tearin'?" or where the conglomerated elements of its subluminated greatness cum from? The answer comes from Lexington, from spunky Bunker Hill, and travels down the rugged road of time from the Fourth of July, 1776, down to the present hour—a stoppin' occasionally to view the onward march of American gullory, in the truly sublime, incomparably patriotic, and thunderingly independent sights that annually meet the gaze of the descendants of those heroes, whose deeds stand like gigantic rocky barriers in the fundamental, political, elemental, ornamental and regimental Thermopylæ of the nation: Sights that make the foes of freedom to look cross-eyed, and the whole great American world of Yankee-doodledom to rejoice, as did Joshua of old, after he had got the children of Israel and their parents across the Rocky Mountains, safely "on the other side of Jordan:" Sights that makes every school-boy feel like a *hero*, and every school-girl a *shero*—the great and glorious custom of *Malishy General Trainin'*. For the militia is the bone and gristle of the country. It locks, bars, and bolts the gates of all American creation, and stands sentinel on the tallest ramparts of Yankee-Doodle's circumlocutory dominions.

This Republic would be a miserable institution, but for the militia. It keeps the ardent spirits of civil and military effulgence, of which all drink deeply, in a glow, or unrestrained ferocity, and *shets pan* on the fillibustering propensities of hot-headed regulars, whose effervescing patriotism stirs up the bad blood of that enthusiastic state of pugnacity and reckless go-ahead-ativeness, so common to all that portion of mankind, who do not and never did belong to the militia. Folks that call it a farce, don't see the glory of the future, nor they don't dream of the postmortem fame our ancestors are sure to experience, in the militia services of their country's defence, a fightin' the foe, and a dyin' for their country's good.

There ain't a more patriotically glorious sight to be seen than a militia commander in full military canonicals, with gilt buttons all the way down onto the front of his coat, from his chin to his stummick—a silk bandanna pocket-handkerchief put into his rejuvinescent bosom, to wipe off the inspirations of glory, and the perspiration of sweat from his pusillanimous brow—a wearin' a red sash around the mortal circumference of his military dimensions—a bearin' on his shoulders the military tokens of greatness and gallory and high distinction—a sword hangin' restless at his side, a waitin' for something awful to "turn up"—his coat-tail a shinin' with stars, and his log scabbard streaked with stripes runnin' up and down lengthways—his cap containin' a red and pumpkin-colored feather stuck into it onto the top of his head—the red bein' symbelmatical of his heart's blood, and the pumpkin-color his coming from a farm, like General Sinsinnattus from Ohio, at his country's call. The sight of such a man, amounted on the back of a demented gray war-horse, fully caparisoned in all the catouteraments, pomp, epiphany, and circumstantial pride of gallorious war—who scents villainous salt-petre in the breeze, sees the brittlin' bayonets a shinin' in the sunshine, hears the roarin' of the six-pounders, "whose rude clamors the immortal Jove's dread thunders" can't begin to counterfeit—a pawin' the earth as if he'd dig a hole to bury his country's foes in, without the benefit of clergy—a neighin' like thunder, and hard to hold—a tearin' round the field on a general trainin', a shoutin' out his orders just as loud as he can holler—as Shakspeare says in his Pilgrim's Progress, "determined to do something, or else die"—a havin' all his commands executed with militia precision and promptness, because as John Bunyan says in the play called "The more you put down, the less you take up," "If it is done when it is finished, then it's best to have it done right away,"—I say the sight of such like is enough to make the whole world join the militia.

I believe the perlucent light of this extemporaneous Republic is borrowed from the militia, and the grit of good government grows out of it; and what's more, I don't believe the Gineral Government could go on without the militia—but with it, our proud motto, "United we understand, but divided we *don't* understand," will last forever.

Look at a few names of distinguished militia heroes. First comes General George Washington, who lived and flourished in this Republic 1776 years ago next Fourth of July; who fit in the revolution agin England, and who every American holds dear in his or her bosom, was a member of the militia. General Putnam was one of 'em, and a tearin' one too. You all remember the darin' account of his performance a ridin' down a steep ledge of rocks, three miles high, on the neck of his war horse, after that noble animal had been disabled, by havin' his long switch tail wound round a young oak saplin, in his speed through the woods, and havin' his back-bone pulled clean out. This, my brave fellow-sogers, fellow-citizens, and friends! was a militia officer, a chasin' up the British. Why, spunk and patriotism stuck out in him, like quills upon the porky-fretfulpine. So, also, did Cæsar, Hannibal, Alexander, Sipryo Africanus, Shakspeare, Boneparte, Falstaff, Santa Anna, and Brigham Young, belong to the militia And so also, my brave comrads, so also, so do I— and I hope if I am ever spared to live long enough to be permitted to die onto the defence of my country's rights, I may die at the head of the 9,999th Regiment, with this good sword drawed on my war horse high in the air, perfectly inconsistent to the bullets of the enemy, and oblivious to nothin' but my country—a fightin' like a polar bear jest ketched, and a lookin' up to the motto of my country's gallorious ensign, " U-pluribus E-num," (which is American Latin, and means, the country's safe, as long as the people be,) with my head surrounded by a cloud of opake glory a bustin' out on every side, and a gazin' on the war-hoop of freedom a rollin' round and round amongst my brave sogers, in tones of thunder and discord, that shall " fright the souls of fearful adversaries to death and destruction"— and calmly take this immaterial military spirit from scenes of strife and fightin' to where the enemy cease from troublin' and the militia are at rest.

Three cheers for the militia in general, and the 9,999th Regiment in particular! Talk of *buyin'* Cuby and payin' cash for it! Why, the 9,999th Regiment can thrash the life out of that half-Spanish, yaller community any forenoon before dinner! and as commanding officer of it, I'd like to contract with Uncle Sam's Gineral Government to take Cuby for fifty thousand dollars, except furnishin' powder and balls and cannon; and as for the feedin' my men, I'll agree to give 'em better clothes and vittles, and more on 'em, than the commissary department usually allows, and for fifty per cent. less than the government Peter Funks do, who git contracts to starve the army, under pretext of feedin' on 'em: and I'll agree to discount ten per cent. from the face of the bill for the ready cash too.

Fellow-citizens! all great national reforms, if only based upon the elemental, fundamental, governmental, and regimental strictness of the gallorious militia, would conduce to the greatest good of the greatest number—provided they belonged to the militia. All orphan asylums should be based upon its gallorious superstructure; and the patriotic ancestors of orphans should be taught that the safety of this growin' Republic requires that the sons of orphan parents should become members of the militia as soon as they come to years of ubiquity.

That all American children, who are agoin' to be born hereafter, under twenty-one years of age, may first see the light and breathe the air of freedom, under a militia dispensation, and be nursed by revolutionary mothers, whose bosoms overflow with lacteal patriotism forever. Then the quiet confidence in all excitements, that spring from a temporary feeling of a positive consciousness of doubtful security, that culminates in the full maturity of something or other—a preparation for anything, with a desire that nothing may prevent it, shall be the great bulwark of everlasting strength in the framework of fortified defence to all who dare to presume to trifle with the constitutional purity of the Goddess of Liberty.

RECITATION.

BY A GIRL.

IN MEMORIAM.

To keep our memories green is my object this evening. Summer and autumn, seed-time and harvest have succeeded each other; and now boisterous winter has covered the earth with its robes of white. The year is mourning the decease of its beauties. The flowers that adorned every valley, and covered each hill-side, have yielded up their lives. The leaves of the forest trees—the sturdy oak and the graceful elm—have withered; and, borne away by the rough winds of autumn, lie decaying beside the fences or in little hillocks by the road-side. The fruits have ripened, each in their season, and have been gathered home, ready for the husbandman's use. All nature has filled its measure of increase, and has rendered to the Creator the results of His bounteous gifts of sunshine and shower bestowed during the passing seasons.

Our Sabbath-school, a spiritual plant, has been maturing also, and some of its fruit have been deemed fitted for the Master's use. Some, that we in our ignorance thought unripe—some that just began life's pilgrimage—God saw had fulfilled their destiny ; and He has called them from duties on earth to joys in heaven. An immortal trio have passed over to the other shore. Three of our number have sank to rest in the Saviour's bosom. We believe that when our voices are sounding forth our beloved songs, their voices are causing the arches of heaven to ring with the lofty refrain—" Hozannah ! hozannah !" They are the first fruits—the harvest offering to our heavenly Father. Some were tender and loved ones : the sacrifices on our part were the greater. Some were of great promise. The ways of Providence are mysterious. All were members of our school. They were our friends, our loved companions ; and we mourn for them. Their names have been enrolled on the tablet of eternity. From them let us each—classmates, schoolmates, teachers and officers—learn that

> "Life is real—life is earnest—
> And the grave is not its goal:
> Dust thou art—to dust returnest,
> Was not written of the soul."

From their example let us profit. Did they love the truth, and seek wisdom ? let us choose the path of virtue, and aim to make the secrets of nature our own. Were they gentle and lovely ? let us be kind and forbearing. Did they love their teachers and playmates ? let us endeavor to be the pride of our school, and the sought companions of the good and true. Did they venerate their parents? let us be assured they had their reward. Were they the lovers of the Saviour? He has gathered them unto His bosom. Their errors we will not remember. The veil of forgetfulness will be drawn,—they are remembered only in their good deeds. From the lesson of their being so early called from life, let us learn to labor while opportunity is given us. Perhaps ere we meet in such a scene as this again, some of us may be called to render an account of our labors here on earth.

> "Time is fleeting:
> And our hearts, though stout and brave,
> Still like muffled drums are beating
> Funeral marches to the grave."

Classmates! Schoolmates! shall we gird ourselves anew for the race we are to run? Shall we determine more diligently to study the chart of life? Shall we enter upon our life-work with more earnestness than ever before? If so, let us invoke the aid of our heavenly Father, and follow constantly the precepts contained in His holy word. So shall our example be bright and shining. So shall we triumph in the hour of release from labor. So shall our memories be evergreen.

ZETA.

RECITATION.

OH, WHY SHOULD THE SPIRIT OF MORTAL BE PROUD?*

Oh, why should the spirit of mortal be proud?
Like a swift, fleeting meteor, a fast-flying cloud,
A flash of the lightning, a break of the wave,
He passeth from life to his rest in the grave.

The leaves of the oak and the willow shall fade,
Be scattered around and together be laid;
And the young and the old, and the low and the high,
Shall moulder to dust and together shall lie.

The infant a mother attended and loved;
The mother that infant's affection who proved;
The husband that mother and infant who blessed,
Each, all, are away to their dwellings of Rest.

The hand of the king that the sceptre hath borne;
The brow of the priest that the mitre hath worn;
The eye of the sage and the heart of the brave,
Are hidden and lost in the depth of the grave.

The peasant, whose lot was to sow and to reap;
The herdsman, who climbed with his goats up the steep;
The beggar who wandered in search of his bread;
Have faded away like the grass that we tread.

The saint who enjoyed the communion of heaven,
The sinner who dared to remain unforgiven,

* A favorite Poem often recited by President Lincoln.

The wise and the foolish, the guilty and just,
Have quietly mingled their bones in the dust.

So the multitude goes, like the shower or the weed
That withers away to let others succeed;
So the multitude comes, even those we behold,
To repeat every tale that has often been told.

For we are the same that our fathers have been;
We see the same sights that our fathers have seen—
We drink the same stream and view the same sun—
And run the same course our fathers have run.

The thoughts we are thinking our fathers would think;
From the death we are shrinking our fathers would shrink;
To the life we are clinging they also would cling;
But it speeds for us all, like a bird on the wing.

They loved, but the story we cannot unfold:
They scorned, but the heart of the haughty is cold;
They grieved, but no wail from their slumber will come;
They joyed, but the tongue of their gladness is dumb.

They died, ay! they died; we things that are now,
That walk on the turf that lies over their brow,
And make in their dwellings a transient abode,
Meet the things that they met on their pilgrimage road.

Yea, hope and despondency, pleasure and pain,
We mingle together in sunshine and rain;
And the smile and the tear, the song and the dirge,
Still follow each other, like surge upon surge.

'Tis the wink of an eye, 'tis the draft of a breath,
From the blossom of health to the paleness of death,
From the gilded saloon to the bier and the shroud—
Oh, why should the spirit of mortal be proud?

ALPHABET OF SHORT RULES.

A ttend well to your own business.
B e punctual in all your engagements.
C onsider well before making promises.
D o right in all things without fear.
E nvy no man his apparent prosperity.
F ret not at disappointments.
G ive liberally to the suffering poor.
H old fast your integrity.
I nfringe on no man's right.
J udge not others severely.
K eep away from evil company.
L end to those that cannot buy.
M ake no display of your charities.
N ever profess what you do not practice.
O ccupy your time in usefulness.
P ay every one their just dues.
Q uarrel not with your associates.
R emember your dependence on Providence.
S trive to promote the happiness of others.
T reat every one with civility.
U se the things of this world with discretion.
V illify no person's reputation.
W atch against temptation.
X amine your own character.
Y ield not to the persuasion of the vicious.
Z ealously pursue the path of duty.
& hope for everlasting joy.

THE BATTLE OF LIFE.

The battle of life, in by far the greater number of cases, must necessarily be fought UP HILL; and to win it, without a struggle, is perhaps to win it without honor. If there were no DIFFICULTIES, there would be no SUCCESS; if there were nothing to struggle for, there would be nothing to be achieved. Difficulties may intimidate the weak, but they act only as a stimulus to a man of courage and resolution. All experience of life, indeed, serves to prove that the impediments thrown in the way o human advancement, may for the most part be overcome by STEADY GOOD CONDUCT, HONEST ZEAL, ACTIVITY, PERSEVERANCE, and a determined resolution to SURMOUNT DIFFICULTIES. The triumph of the Just is sure!

MODERN SABBATH-SCHOOL ROOM.

MORAL AND RELIGIOUS

Original

MISCELLANIES.

The Last Best Gift.

A HEART-STIRRING SCENE.

[A Christian father, lying upon his death-bed, called his three children to his side, and presented each with a Bible, with the following lines inscribed:]

TO ELIZABETH.

FAREWELL, daughter! I must leave thee—
    Earthly pleasures now are o'er;
May God—'the orphan's God' receive thee
    When you see my face no more.
Let this Book, by kindness given,
    Lead thee, when thy father's dead—
It will guide thee up to heaven,
    Where no farewell tears are shed.

TO JEREMIAH.

A father's gift!—a father's prayer
    Goes with this Book of God—
Embrace its truths—its counsels share—
They'll guard thy feet from many a snare
    When I am 'neath the sod.
A father's gift—the purest—best,
    Dear child! that he can give:
This chart will lead thee into rest,
This compass points thee to the blest,
    That you with Christ may live.

TO FANNY.

Loved one! I must leave thee now,
　　I cannot tarry here—
The dew of death is on my brow,
　　His messenger is near.
I go—but leave this precious boon
　　My Fanny's heart to cheer :
She cannot seek the Lord too soon,
　　Nor God too young revere.
This Book, with holy precepts fraught,
　　Her dying father gives—
Oh! may she in its truths be taught
　　While on the earth she lives ;
And be prepared, when death shall come,
To meet me in yon blissful home.

Written in a Hymn Book.

FAREWELL, Isaac! God direct thee!
　　Make His truth thy chiefest joy---
He mid strangers will protect thee,
　　Let His praise be thy employ.
Oh! may His name thy lips confess,
　　While traveling to the grave---
Then God thy sacrifice will bless,
　　And Isaac he will save.

Farewell Hymn,

TO REV. J. J. SMITH, ON LEAVING HIS CHARGE.

Tune—"*Bavaria.*"

FAREWELL, brother! kindly greetings
    Early told thy welcome here:
Happy since have been our meetings,
    Sweeter, better through each year.
Since we met, our hearts have blended
    In the joyful work of prayer—
Gracious blessings have descended,
    God has kept us in his care.

Zion prospers!—Thanks be given
    To the Saviour for His grace:
Sinners here have heard of heaven,
    And have started in the race.
Precious ones have gone to glory,
    Who were of our little band,—
Oft thou'st heard their hopeful story,
    Often clasped their friendly hand.

Zion prospers!—Long thy teaching,
    Much loved Pastor! may we show—
Long reiterate thy preaching
    With our actions here below.

"Doers of the word" thou'st spoken
  In this temple—fervent—true,—
Then, when life's sweet ties are broken,
  May we sleep in Christ with you.

Zion's shepherd!—God attend thee
  Still thy mission to proclaim,—
May His arm of strength befriend thee,
  As in other years the same.
Go!—the world in sin is lying!
  Tell of mansions—thrones above:
Speak for God! to souls undying,
  Who have never known His love.

Christian soldier! 'mid life's changes
  We will pray for thee and thine:
Time nor distance love estranges—
  Onward! in the cause divine.
Soon, the battle will be ended—
  Soon, the victor's crown be won:
Jesus waits, with arms extended,
  To reward His faithful son.

Epitaph.

Rest thee, dear wife! awhile in sleep—
  Life's toilsome journey has an end!
This grave thy precious dust will keep—
  Eternity with Jesus spend:
We soon will come with thee to rest,
Wife—mother—sister—with the blest.

Impromptu Lines,

WRITTEN ON A COFFIN-LID—WHILE WATCHING A CORPSE.

I know this corpse! these eyes now dark
    Have often smiled on me,—
Death must have loved so fair a mark,
To close so soon this kindled spark
    Struck from Divinity.

I know this corpse! this silent tongue
    Has often called my name,—
With those of mine, as frail and young,
Oft has he laughed, and played, and sung,
    And they yet live the same!

I know this corpse! this lovely boy!
    The pride of many eyes—
This dust was once a mother's joy—
For him was toil made sweet employ,
    And fervent prayers would rise.

Here lies a father's hope—a son,
    On whom his heart was set:
We've coffined up his only one—
Ere six short years a race is run
    He never can forget.

To future years his eyes were cast,
    To Manhood's strength and prime—

But God's swift angel flying past,
Thought this had better be the last,
   And took him up from Time.

And who, dear parents! knows the best,
   His Maker—God—or thee?
Would ye awake him from his rest—
Recall his spirit from the blest,
   Now ransomed, pure and free?

Like Bible-David, weep no more
   Now that the child is dead—
From pain released, and suff'ring o'er,
He's gained the clime and reached the shore
   Where Henrietta fled.

Grieve not, ye stricken! "all is well"—
   This tie is only riven
To mind you where the good will dwell,
To woo the heart, and break the spell
   That clouds a view of heaven.

Acrostic.

J oy—joy to thy spirit! escaped from its clay!
E nter now into rest—to yon mansions away!
N or mourning—nor sorrow—can longer molest,
N or more shall thy bosom with grief be opprest.
E nough---come up higher---life's journey is run,
T he grave hath received thee---the victory's won---
T ime closes---Eternity now has begun.

Anniversary Ode.

FOR "THE UNITED DAUGHTERS OF AMERICA."

America's Daughters! in Friendship united
    Together assemble each other to cheer,---
By their watchword of "Union" the States are invited
    To link in the chain with an object so dear.
With heart and with hand for our Country's protection,
    We welcome her Daughters of Virtue and Truth—
Who, reared in the homes of our freeborn connection,
    Have learned its true value in childhood and youth.

Columbia's Daughters! fair Freedom's descendants!
    Ye matrons and maidens of Patriot sires!
Your charter—your altar—is proud independence—
    And here you may dwell till her Eagle expires.
Let Liberty's triumphs your children be learning,
    And tell of the foes who invaded our shore—
Thus, early instruction will keep the flame burning
    That dwelt in the hearts of our fathers of yore.

America's Daughters! in Friendship united!
    We'll cherish each other in sickness or health,—
The rosebloom of womanhood soon may be blighted,
    And Love may be called for her Pity and Wealth.
Then, then with the free hand of Plenty enlighten
    The bosom of sorrow—the heart full of care;
And Sympathy's kind voice the dim eye will brighten
    Ere heaven is opened its freedom to share.

To the First-Born.

Sweet, guileless boy! my muse for thee
    A simple note would raise—
A prayer that thou may'st ever be
From Sin's polluting power free,
    And kept in Wisdom's ways.

The world may lure and charm thine eye
    With all its glitt'ring toys:
Yet soon will earthly pleasures fly—
There's nothing sure beneath the sky,
    And transient are our joys.

Oh! I could wish thou ne'er should'st know
    Affliction-- sorrow---pain:
That heaven would blessings rich bestow,
And guard thy steps, in weal or wo,
    Till dust joins dust again.

I would that angels pure and bright
    Their vigils round would keep---
And watch thee in Misfortune's night,
When clouds are dark, or storms affright,
    To lull thy breast to sleep.

Learn, early learn the Lord to fear,
    His just commands obey;
'Twill serve to make thee happy here---
'Twill banish grief when Death comes near,
    And take its sting away.

'Twill lead thee to unfading bowers,
   Where youth will ever bloom;
Where all is love, and deathless flowers
Surround God's friends, who erst were ours---
   'Tis life beyond the tomb.

Stanzas to a Bride.

Trav'ler to a world untried,
   By mortal never trod—
Would'st thou have a faithful guide
   To lead thee home to God?
This precious volume be thy chart,
   This Lamp to light thee, take;
Oh! keep its precepts in thy heart
   For the Redeemer's sake.

May the companion of thy youth,
   The partner of thy choice,
Be guided by this Word of Truth,
   And by its warning voice,—
That both at last may sweetly share
   The joys of life above—
And may the donor meet you there
   To praise redeeming love.

Valedictory Hymn.

DEDICATED TO A PASTOR ON LEAVING HIS CHARGE.

Brother beloved! a kind farewell
    We breathe for thee to-day—
Our hearts with sad emotions swell
    The parting word to say.
Thy work is done—thy mission ends—
    The faithful charge is given:
Oh! may our union here as friends,
    Be sweeter still in heaven.

How brief the years since first thy voice
    Within these walls was heard!
How many since in Christ rejoice,
    And love the Living Word!
'Tis not in vain thou'st labored here,
    In feebleness of frame—
More precious fruit may yet appear,
    To bless our pastor's name.

And is it past? Shall we no more
    Thy pious counsels share?
Are all our social meetings o'er
    Of melody and prayer?
Yes, we must part! those sacred hours
    Of fellowship must close—
Perchance till we, in Eden bowers,
    From earthly ills repose.

Thence onward, brother! press thy way,
    God's enemies pursue—
The Master calls—His voice obey—
    Behold! a crown in view.
Aloud proclaim "the day of grace"—
    The Gospel trumpet sound;
Wage war with sin in every place
    Where sinners may be found.

Strong be thy heart to do His will,
    His service to perform,—
May love for souls thy bosom fill,
    And keep it ever warm.
For others' good we bid thee Go—
    Diffuse the holy fire—
Preach CHRIST to dying men below,
    Till He shall call thee higher.

"Fire! Fire!"

ON THE NINTH WARD PUBLIC SCHOOL CALAMITY.*

Hark! a bell for fire is pealing,
    Where a thousand children meet—
Dread alarm! more dread revealing!
    As they rush from that retreat.

See! a scene the most appalling!
    Infants to the vortex run!
Death stands near to wait their falling—
    Mangled corses! life is done!

Hark! what sounds of woe are stealing,
  Sad and fearful, on the ear!
Waking every chord of feeling—
  Starting from each eye the tear!

See! yon streets with frantic mothers!
  Pale with grief, they run and cry,—
Sisters in pursuit of brothers---
  Brothers to the rescue fly!

Who may soothe the hearts yet breaking
  O'er the memories of this day?
Fifty loved ones home forsaking,
  To return---cold, breathless clay!

"Good by, mother! I am going!"
  "School-time, mother dear---good bye!"
Cheerful steps, and hearts o'erflowing,
  To the fatal spot they hie!

Children of the homes we cherish!
  Native-born! your loss we feel:
Thus in early youth to perish,
  Fills with grief the common weal.

Saviour! soothe the mourners weeping
  O'er these graves of buried love;
Take, oh! take them in Thy keeping,
  Till they re-unite above.

---

* In New-York City, Nov. 20, 1851, at which time fifty-three of the scholars were taken to their homes dead.

Tribute of Affection,

ON THE DEATH OF MRS. SARAH H. B******.

Rest, Sarah, rest! entombed in earth
    Thy lovely form is sleeping—
Whilst kindred hearts, who knew thy worth,
    In anguish deep are weeping.
Fond Mem'ry comes—a faithful guest!
    Youth's cloudless scenes recalling;
And leaning on Affection's breast,
    The tears of both are falling.

It seems but yesterday, in prayer
    We saw thee humbly kneeling—
For grace life's parting hour to bear
    In accents soft appealing:
And then methought the change was near,
    The wheel would soon be broken—
Our meetings close forever here,
    Our farewell soon be spoken.

We are bereft. Thy vacant seat
    Oft tells the cheering story,
That though in time we shall not meet,
    We soon will meet in glory.
We part a little while, 'tis true—
    A few short years we sever;
The blissful courts that welcome you,
    Shall be our home forever.

Then wherefore o'er her grave repine,
    Companion—child—and mother?
The form ye to the dust consign,
    Shall rise in Christ another;
Her heart's desire—her constant trust—
    To whom her youth was given—
And though ye coffin up her dust,
    She lives with Him in heaven.

Then wherefore linger, brothers! friends!
    O'er your buried treasure?
Angelic bands her flight attends
    To blood-bought, deathless pleasure.
Hark! dear classmates! she is calling—
    Onward—upward—to thy Love!
Many from our ranks are falling,
    To increase the Church above.

Epitaph.

Sleep on, my wife! my Margaret dear!
No earthly ills can reach you here—
From this green grave thy dust shall rise,
And meet thy loved ones in the skies—
When Christ again from Heaven shall come
To call His ransomed children home.

Temperance Ode.

"WASHINGTON UNION, DAUGHTERS OF TEMPERANCE."

Hail, Washington Daughters! your Nation's defender!
    The iron-souled chieftain! America's pride!
In the forerank of battle, where cowards surrender,
    Undaunted he stood, till he conquered or died.
Tho' the foe compass'd round, and brave hearts were fearing
    Unyielding in duty, our Washington stands,---
He fought for the Right, and while Justice was cheering,
    Redeem'd his loved Country from Tyranny's hands.

Then crown him, ye Daughters! with plaudits receive him,
    The "good and the brave" your example should be---
Thus garlands of glory again you may weave him,
    By keeping his children from Alcohol free.
A yoke is upon them, which soon must be broken,
    Than kingly oppression more galling and base:
Else Liberty's name with tears may be spoken,
    And her Eagle will fly from our shores in disgrace.

Advance, then, ye Matrons! ye Maidens and Daughters!
    Your influence give the poor drunkard to save,---
The foeman may scorn at our Croton's pure waters,
    And fall, ere his time, in a dishonored grave.
'Tis yours to regain and direct the benighted,
    The children of sorrow and want to reclaim:
Then husbands and brothers shall rise up delighted.
    And bless the kind sisters with Washington's name.*

---

* Their Banner represented Washington crossing the bridge at Trenton, N. J., Dec. 26, 1776.

To a Wedded Couple.

"Remember 'tis no common tie
    That binds your youthful heart;
'Tis only one that truth should weave,
    And only death can part."

Art thou wed? And was it spoken,
    "I pronounce you man and wife?"
May thy vows remain, unbroken,
    Through the future of thy life.
Was it Love, sincere, confiding,
    Bade thee give thy hand away?
Oh! may it be strong, abiding,
    As upon thy marriage day.

Now the world looks bright before thee—
    Hope has lit his torch anew;
Cloudless skies are smiling o'er thee—
    Happy voices greet thee too.
Kindred friends look on approving—
    Kind good wishes fill thy ear;
And thy husband, fond and loving,
    Whispers words the heart to cheer.

I could wish it were so ever—
    Naught to cloud thy coming years;
I could wish thou mayest never
    Feel a sorrow meet for tears.

But, alas! no mortal knoweth
    What events await us here—
God alone true peace bestoweth,
    Seek his favor—love and fear.

The Future.

TO MISS J. R. C.

Oh! brightly seems the coming year,
    And gay the scenes around---
Sweet voices greet thy youthful ear,
    Like music's varied sound.
The eye of Friendship clearly beams,
    And hearts for thee are true—
While Hope in Fancy's early dreams,
    New pleasures bring to view.

But ah! young friend! to care unknown,
    Each joy may flee away—
Thy hours of gladness have an end,
    And sorrows cloud thy day.
'Tis changing all beneath the sky,
    There's nothing certain here—
The loveliest flowers will fade and die,
    And beauty disappear.

JANUARY.

Farewell Hymn.

TO REV. WM. H. JOHNSON, ON LEAVING HIS CHARGE.

Tune—" *Alida.*"

Servant of God! our pastor-friend!
　We meet to bid adieu—
Thy work of love with us must end,
　Though faithful, kind, and true.
Thy mission like a dream appears,
　So quickly has it flown—
And yet, within the two brief years,
　How much each heart has known!

Thou cam'st when Death, throughout the land,
　In triumph passed along,—
We've seen thee by the dying stand,
　And in the fun'ral throng.
Beside the mourners, in their grief,
　Thy voice was often heard,
Inviting all to seek relief
　In Jesus and his Word.

Here, too, within this sacred place,
　Where oft times we have met,
We've seen such rapture in thy face,
　We never may forget.
In accents chaste, and full of love,
　Thy exhortations came—
And converts—seeking 'crowns above'—
　Are here to bless thy name.

Our Pastor leaves his flock to-day,
    In the Great Shepherd's care,—
Oh! may He guide thy devious way
    His Gospel to declare:
Make plain thy path—His grace bestow,
    And grant thee years of peace—
Till, brought where joys eternal flow,
    This changeful life shall cease.

God speed thee, brother! firmly stand!
    The blood-stained Cross defend,—
Take the bless'd Bible in thy hand,
    And show mankind their Friend.
Our pray'rs for thee shall still arise,
    Though absent from our sight—
Till, joining hands in yonder skies,
    The Christian host unite.

Stanza.

Give my love to the wedded pair,
    And wish them joy for me—
Tell them I wish I had been there ,
    The bride and groom to see.
Long life be theirs—a happy life,
    With every comfort blest—
May Ada prove a faithful wife,
    And Willie's heart find rest.

The Sunbeams of Spring.

WRITTEN ON BROOKLYN HEIGHTS.

Hail! hail to the sunbeams of morn
    That break from yon redolent sky—
O'erspreading each valley and lawn,
    Where winter terrific passed by.
The "day-star" in beauty comes forth,
    Effulgent with life-giving beams—
Subverting the winds of the North,
    And melting the ice-bounded streams.

Flow on, gentle river! in pride—
    Come home, little warblers of Spring!
Awhile with my loved one reside,
    And here with my favorite sing.—
Come, bring the sweet olives of peace,
    Ye songsters and birds of the grove:
Let anthems of music increase,
    And praise to our Father above.

The earth with sweet fragrance is rife,
    And flow'rets will soon be in view;
The shrub, vine, and tree shoot to life,
    Bedecked with the rain-drop and dew:
The mountains, the hills, and the vales,
    With greenness be carpeted o'er—
Fresh odors and spice from the vales
    Ascend to the God we adore.

Oh! welcome again is the Spring!
    And welcome mild Phœbus, whose light
O'er nature a brightness doth fling,
    And cheers the dark wintry blight.
I hail thee, sweet sunbeam! with joy—
    Great source of all blessings here given;
May gratitude be our employ,
    Till Spring buds around us in heaven.

Dedication for an Album.

DEAR sister mine! I bring to thee
    This token of a brother's love---
Affection's casket let it be,
Forever fraught with Purity,
Rays from the heart, which all may see,
    Like silent stars which shine above.

'Tis Friendship's gift! 'tis Friendship's shrine,
    A record of the gems of Mind:
I would each pen to Truth incline,
Each prayer for thee be warm as mine---
May Virtue's hand guide every line,
    With thought sincere, and chaste and kind.

Our Child is Gone!

Our child is gone! the rose is dead!
    How short—how fleet its bloom!
The grass is springing o'er its head
    While mould'ring in the tomb.
A mother's love could not withhold
    Its Maker's high behest—
But ere Misfortune, dark and cold,
    Had crossed its tender breast,
He took it from her clasping arms,
With all its smiling, mortal charms:

Alas! sweet, innocent, and mild,
    Ere three brief years it fell—
And now she's mother to a child
    Where seraph spirits dwell.
Transplanted to the Eden land,
    It lives to bloom again;
And nourished by a kinder hand,
    'Twill know no grief or pain:
But flourish in the bowers above,
    The clime of bliss—the home of love.

Our child is gone! her voice no more
    May break upon the ear;
Her lightsome step across the floor
    We may no longer hear.
Each little toy she's left behind
    Familiar to her sight—
But joys, beyond the finite mind,
    Are now her soul's delight:
And soon, dear parents! ye may rise
To join your babe beyond the skies.

Responsive Address,

ON THE RECEPTION OF A BEAUTIFUL PICTURE, MADE BY THE HANDS OF TWELVE LADIES.

At a Sabbath-School Anniversary.

LADIES OF THE SABBATH-SCHOOL :—It would require the eloquence of a Stockton or a Summerfield to express the feelings which have influenced my heart during the delivery of your Presentation Address. They have made me wish for the possession of a tongue capable of giving voice to the thoughts of the soul. But this ability I lack, and confess, in the offset of my remarks, that Fowler says I am deficient in "freedom of speech." What I wish to say, however, will more interest these little boys and girls than their kind teachers: I remember, children, when the first Sabbath-School was opened on Long Island. It was in the year 1821. [How long ago was it, boys?] Yes, forty years have gone into eternity—forty Christmas days have passed away since then! I knew a little boy who was a member of that School—who was present when the first prayer was offered and the first hymn was sung. It was the custom in those days for the children to march from the school-house to the church—and it was a beautiful sight to see that happy, cheerful company, going hand in hand, two by two, through the streets to the temple of God—headed by a white-haired, kind-hearted man for its Superintendent, and the teachers walking by their sides. I have often seen the children of the Roman Catholic Church walking in this manner in New-York city, and have been reminded of the youthful days of that little boy. He was a constant attendant of his Sabbath-School for about five years, when a serious accident happened to him. It was in this wise:—One afternoon he took his kite, and, climbing upon a high pile of wood, raised it in the air. While witnessing his kite floating in the breeze, he forgot he was standing upon "slippery places." Those sticks moved from under his feet, and he kept moving backward and backward,—but directly he fell to the ground. The alarm was given by a man from a window; and after removing about a load of wood, as I was told, he was found—mangled and bleeding profusely. A hand-barrow was brought to convey him to the nearest drug-store—but, while passing through the street, a little girl saw him, and exclaimed: "I know that little boy—he is a member of my Sunday-School," and told where he lived. He was carried home to an afflicted mother, and she a widow. Dr. Mott came from New-York, and four other physicians were called in. It was soon found that his arm was broken, and the skull terribly fractured—from which was taken a piece of bone as large as the palm of your hand, and splintered into nine pieces. For three months that poor little boy lay in a state of unconsciousness—his shroud was prepared, and I was told his coffin selected. It was needful that night-watchers should attend him—and who do you think they were? I will tell you—they were his Sabbath-School teachers. When the whole number had taken their turns, they commenced again. And not only did they perform this kindness, but all came with little presents or tokens of sympathy in their hands, to minister to the little sufferer's comfort. Strange to say that little boy lived!— God gave his angel charge concerning him. In about a year he returned to his Sabbath-School. He lived to bury that dear, kind mother, who had nursed him day and night through all this trying period. He lived to become a Sabbath-School teacher, librarian and superintendent. He lived to stand beside the grave of that venerable white-haired man who had been his Superintendent in youth; and to-night he stands before you, ladies, to return you his hearty thanks for your kind consideration. I was that little boy.

Be pleased, Miss D******, to convey to your associates the pleasure I feel in receiving their token of approval. I will place it upon the walls at home, and leave it to my children to remind them that their father had friends in this Sabbath-School.

Ministers of Jesus! ambassadors of his Gospel! before I take my seat let me repeat to you His commandment— "Feed my lambs." It encourages teachers and children to see their minister frequently in the Sabbath-School room. I have often thought, if I filled a minister's office in the providence of God, I would get the love of the children by my care of them. If I wished to raise a church and increase its membership, I would devote much time to its Sabbath-School interests. Oh, my brethren! Ministers, let this night's scenes give a new impulse to your hearts to act for the salvation of the little ones, and God will bless you—parents will bless you—and they will bless you when they meet you in the judgment!

www.ingramcontent.com/pod-product-compliance
Lightning Source LLC
Chambersburg PA
CBHW020239240426

43672CB00006B/578